THROUGH MY EYES

CHANGES TO THE EDITION

This is Ella Simon's book, so the only changes are ones she would have wanted.

The photographs worried her and she just couldn't find the ones she was after. For this edition, those elusive photographs have become available through Mr Jim Revitt of the Australian Broadcasting Commission, a former resident of the district. His research led to the publication of three books of photographs, *The Good Old Days*, published by Anvil Press. Jim granted permission to reproduce from his books. About Ella Simon he wrote, 'She was an impressive person; I will never forget a lovely morning tea I had with her one day when she recounted so much of the past and identified so many people in the photographs. I am delighted that her excellent work is to be reprinted.'

Ella was not happy with the original Foreword and this has been replaced by one that she did like. It originally appeared as a book review in the *Sydney Morning Herald* and Les Murray has generously rewritten that article for this edition. He also suggested adding the Afterword, about how the book came to be written, and helped with its creation.

Ella's family and friends helped with the chapter on her death and funeral, which was very hard to write.

Where mistakes have been pointed out, several of the stories have been rewritten. Some have also been expanded. Ella's original text was used.

Mrs Faith Saunders, a close relative of Ella Simon, has given much time to this edition. All changes and additions have been worked out with her help and advice.

AUTHORS DEDICATION

This book is dedicated to my grandmother, who taught me about being both Aboriginal and Christian and who cared so much for all people; and to my father for his honesty with the people he knew he had wronged. It has been made possible through my faith in God who enables me to love.

THROUGH MY EYES

ELLA SIMON

Collins Dove

Published by Collins Dove
60-64 Railway Road,
Blackburn, Victoria 3130
Telephone (03) 877 1333

This edition first published 1987
Reprinted 1989
Cover design by Lisa Lambert

Typeset in 11/12 Times by Solo Typesetting, South Australia
Printed in Australia by The Book Printer

The National Library of Australia
Cataloguing-in-Publication Data:

Simon, Ella 1902-81
    Through my eyes

    New ed.
    ISBN 0 85924 460 1.

    1. Simon, Ella 1902-81 [2]. Aborigines, Australian –
    Mixed bloods – Biography. [3] Aborigines, Australian –
    New South Wales – Taree – Social conditions. I. Title.

305.8'9915'099442

The first edition of this book (1978) was published with the
assistance of the Aboriginal Arts Board of the
Australia Council.

CONTENTS

FOREWORD

In the early 1960s the Swedish linguist Nils Holmer visited the various Aboriginal settlements around the lower north coast of New South Wales, Purfleet on the Manning River, Burnt Bridge and Bellbrook near Kempsey, making the first really detailed study, in modern scientific terms, of Kattang and Thangatti, the ancient languages of the region. One of his informants was the late Mrs Ella Simon, the author of this book.

Kattang was once spoken from the Hunter River in the south to the Hastings in the north, and when Holmer did his research he was able to find ten reasonably good informants, older people who spoke the language with fair fluency, and even some old men who had undergone high-order initiations. This was more than a century and a quarter after white settlement had begun in the region, and it is likely that not one white person in ten thousand living there had the faintest idea that anything of the old culture and its language still survived. We were indifferent, or at the very best shyly diffident, about anything to do with the black people and we allowed injustice to be done to them in our name and behind our back.

Now, sadly, all of Nils Holmer's informants on the Kattang language are dead. The last of the ten to die was

Mrs Simon. In the last years of her life, however, she dictated the material which this book comprises. It is probable that much in it is recorded nowhere else. I only wish she had given us a longer book and put down more of the old lore. There is an essential difference, after all, between material gathered by white scholars from early accounts written down, often in a sketchy way, by white newcomers alien to the culture they are commenting upon and living details described from within the culture itself. Even the degree to which the old culture survives in the altered, much-adapted circumstances of our own day can only really be revealed by one who has a place within it.

Of course, this is not to say that the late Mrs Simon was a fragile museum piece; some hapless seekers after knowledge found that out quite smartly. She was a vigorous, sensible woman of great character and, as her book shows, she had a great deal to record apart from the ancient traditions. Among much else, she was almost certainly the first Aboriginal woman to have been made a Justice of the Peace in Australia. She obtained this position in order to carry on more effectively her fight for better conditions for her people at Purfleet. And it was an effective fight; no one interested in the Aboriginal struggle should fail to read her account of it. It is part of a whole pattern of similar battles carried on all over Australia, battles so often led by women, by which many Aboriginal people have regained their pride and obtained at least some standing in their native country.

Mrs Simon's account is all the more interesting in that it relates to the period of silence before black radicalism and effective publicity for the Aboriginal cause. It belongs, too, to the period of so-called caste, when Aboriginal people were often treated in bewilderingly different ways, by black and white alike, according to the degree of European admixture in their ancestry. Mrs Simon gained a lifelong aversion to the 'colour bar' through being rejected at times by both races. As a light-skinned woman, she knew the pain of being told by some Aboriginal people to go and live in Taree with the other whites, at a time when she would not have been allowed by law to do so. And she knew the bitter pain of white contempt, and cruel rejection by her white father's respectable family. The details are in her book and make chilling reading. In the midst of so much pain, it is good to read that her father himself never rejected her. Equally moving is her tribute to her Aboriginal grandmother who instilled in Ella Simon her own profound Christian faith along with her deep knowledge of traditional language and custom; this wise woman was undoubtedly the strongest influence on Mrs Simon's life. She would need all the resources of Christianity and character to withstand, and eventually to forgive, the savage ironies of her position.

In a way, this book is centrally concerned with irony. Among the many things I learned from it, when I read the first edition in the late 1970s, was the fact that perhaps the worst years of oppression were those from the Depression up until the 1950s, the years when the State Government, rather than the earlier Church Missions, ran the Aboriginal settlements and ruled those who lived on them under monstrously discriminatory laws. It is so common, this tendency in Australia for legislators to take advantage of popular apathy and frame laws which arrogate to government powers far in excess of any real need. Under the Aborigines Protection Act and Regulations, supposedly brought in to benefit the black people, their children could be taken away from them on a white official's say-so, they could be confined to the settlement in which they lived, they were forbidden to travel without permission, forbidden to enter a hotel, disqualified from managing their own financial affairs and barred from most kinds of government employment. Similar laws exist in Queensland even today. In 1957, after years of living under such restrictions, Mrs Simon was granted a Certificate of Exemption, the infamous so-called 'dog licence'. This sickening document is reproduced in her book.

In earlier times Aborigines were certainly discriminated against, to the point of murder and massacre in the very earliest days—Mrs Simon mentions the infamous mass poisonings at Belbora and Soldiers Point. But at least the oppression was sporadic, unorganised, full of exceptions and special arrangements. Aboriginals were adapting to the new world of farms and European work. Some Aboriginal men married white women and some mixed-race families had their own small farms, or some piece of land set aside for them by relatives or friends among the white settlers. Old men whom we would now call traditional owners sometimes lived out their lives in camps set up on a corner of a paddock in their Dreaming country.

If the wish of the white people's elected governments was that the native people should assimilate and disappear, they certainly went about their covert purpose in the wrong way when they separated them from the mainstream and destroyed their incipient adaptation. It is perhaps a final irony that oppressive laws helped to preserve them as a separate group which would one day make separatist demands, sometimes in terms which sadden people of Mrs Simon's generation. But it would be highly pre-sumptuous of me to comment on internal Aboriginal politics. I am much more warmly concerned to pay tribute to one who was, by anyone's standards, clearly one of the great people of my native region. It is good too, finally, that Mrs Simon was assisted in preparing her book by a member of one of the old settler families of our region; that would have been very much in tune with Mrs Simon's own vision of how Australians should live together in our common country. She was, after all, a relation of ours too—and that is a fact which would once have made some settler families nervous, to their very great shame.

LES A. MURRAY

HISTORY OF THE PURFLEET MISSION

Ella Simon's grandparents and a few other families moved to the site in 1902 and the Government, through the Aborigines Protection Board, set aside 12 acres as a reserve. A resident missionary was sent from Sydney by the United Aborigines Mission, one of the inter-denominational missions working in New South Wales and expanding into other parts of Australia as areas became accessible.

Apart from their own houses they built a church, a school, and a Mission house, and these became the nucleus of the settlement and a centre to which the few still living in the bush could come.

They mostly looked after themselves with help from the missionaries and some local help. Work was plentiful then in country areas.

The Depression changed this situation, with an increasing need for welfare and a subsequent increase in numbers on the reserve. The Board's policy changed and a new type of station was created. A Manager was appointed in 1932 with the extra powers the Board had assumed to 'concentrate on reserves, people of Aboriginal blood, with definite control over them ... and they were not to be at liberty to leave without permission' (Aborigines Protection Board Report, 1932). One of the controls they exercised was over all welfare. The area was extended to 51 acres.

The Mission remained a focal point, the church being moved off the reserve to maintain its independence from these restrictions. A lot of the work was done by the Aboriginal people who developed their own leaders and pastors.

Official policy changed again in 1941 to 'assimilation' and the Protection Board was reconstituted as the Welfare Board. This resulted in the 1950s in the closing of the segregated schools and the introduction, to approved individuals who applied, of a type of 'identity card' giving them freedom of movement and access to places from which New South Wales law had banned them, such as hotels.

The 1960s saw renewed activity, this time involving organisations such as C.W.A., Apex, the pre-school movement, and a combined effort to start a shop selling Aboriginal artefacts.

The Referendum in 1967, with its rare and overwhelming 'yes' vote, brought further changes at the bureaucratic level, the Welfare Board being replaced by the Housing Commission (to be responsible for building) and the Department of Child Welfare and Social Welfare (to be responsible for necessary welfare). By then all pensions were being paid direct to those eligible. This meant the end of the rule by Managers at Purfleet; the last one was instructed to leave in 1968.

The Mission had to retrench staff to concentrate on less-accessible areas and withdrew its workers in 1971.

With all of these changes many people left to find work in the cities, unemployment being worse in the country. Some moved into Taree.

The reserve is now owned and administered by a co-operative — the Purfleet Aboriginal Advancement League.

ELLA SIMON

Probably the first Aboriginal woman to be made a J.P., Ella Simon was born in 1902. Her mother was a part-Aboriginal and her father was white; they were not married and her grandparents reared her as their own child. However, her real father, in her words, 'didn't desert her'.

She left Purfleet to work in Sydney in the 1920s, went back to nurse her dying grandmother and, after her grandmother's death, married and settled at Purfleet.

Ella Simon has fought against the petty bureaucratic restrictions imposed on her because of her 'Aboriginal blood' and yet, at the same time, she has been torn between two races and felt that she was not really wanted by either race.

Her efforts succeeded in cutting through many of these restraining factors and, in the 1960s, she was the leader in starting a C.W.A. branch, a pre-school, and a gift shop on the reserve. She was made a J.P. in June 1962.

Basic to her philosophy on life, and her attitude, is her Christian faith which she gleaned from her Aboriginal grandmother at the same time that she learned Aboriginal lore. In her view the two, used correctly, are complementary.

This philosophy has enabled her to be objective in the telling of her story, and to accept people for what they

xiii

are and not for what they look like — as *she* has always wanted to be accepted.

In her 'retirement' she has continued her dedicated church work and many people from both races seek her help and the benefit of her wisdom. Being the last of her generation to know first-hand the Aboriginal language and legends from her part of Australia, she is also sought after by anthropologists, linguists, and educationists — that is, when she is not helping her grandchildren or minding her great-grandchildren. Mrs Simon died in 1981.

NEW SOUTH WALES GOVERNMENT
ABORIGINES PROTECTION ACT, 1909-1943, SECTION 18c.
[REGULATION 56]

CERTIFICATE OF EXEMPTION
From Provisions of the Act and Regulations

THIS IS TO CERTIFY that ....Ella Simon,....

..light Aborigine, aged ..55.. years, residing at ..Aboriginal Station, Taree
(Caste)
is a person who in the opinion of the Aborigines Welfare Board, ought no longer be subject
to the following-provisions ..provisions.. of the Aborigines Protection Act and Regulations, or any of such provisions, and he/she is accordingly exempted from such provisions:—

Issued in compliance with the Resolution of the Aborigines Welfare Board and dated the
..Seventeenth.. day of ..October.., 1957.

Photograph of
Ella Simon

........Chairman.
........Member.
of the Aborigines Welfare Board.
Countersigned by
The Secretary

82595 8-54 A. H. PETTIFER, GOVERNMENT PRINTER

'I had to have this Certificate of Exemption. I had to be recommended to have it. I had to have it to go to any place from which an Aboriginal was banned, to take government jobs, and to leave the reserve. I could never work this out, in spite of my fight for rights. I had to have this piece of paper, like a passport, to give me rights in my own land; to be a citizen of Australia — my own country. My husband got one, too.

xiv

'A Manager once said to an uncle of mine that the Aboriginal was really nobody — not a human being in the land which should have been his own by right of birth.

'I was born here, so I am, in my own right, an "Australian". But, at fifty-five years of age I had to fill in a form to get this "passport" to become a citizen with individual rights. It stank in my nostrils!

'It didn't help either. It meant that we couldn't get a house on the reserve when the house we were living in off the reserve was sold. That is how I came to be living in the old school house — it belonged to the Education Department and not to the Board. Then the Housing Commission took over, told me my house wasn't up to their standards and that I had to leave my home. They condemned the house, so I had to go. I had no choice.

'It also meant that I was allowed to go into hotels but, as I didn't drink, I didn't use this "privilege", thank you.'

ACKNOWLEDGEMENTS IN THE FIRST EDITION OF THIS BOOK (1978)

Many people and organisations have helped and supported me and I thank them all. I would particularly like to thank Alan Cowan who, as in the past, has given me so much of his professional time and advice; and Anne Ruprecht, a friend for many years, who encouraged me in the first place to set down the story of my life and who has helped me throughout the project and done much of the research.

I would also like to thank the Aboriginal Arts Board of the Australia Council for their assistance in the writing and publishing of this book.

ELLA SIMON

CHRONOLOGY OF RELEVANT EXTRACTS FROM N.S.W. ABORIGINES PROTECTION BOARD REPORTS

1883 Aborigines Protection Board established, the chairman being the Inspector-General of Police

1903 Children not permitted to attend Government schools if a 'European' parent objected
The Federal Government forbade employment in Post Offices and the sugar industry

1909 Aborigines Protection Act made into law the powers the Board had been exercising. All reserves, including gift lands, to be taken over by the Board. It had power over the movement of all Aborigines. The Act was later amended to increase this power
Children — special powers were given to remove children from their parents without proof that they were 'neglected'. They were to be 'removed from unsatisfactory surroundings, trained . . . placed in suitable situations'; the 'apprentice system'. Cootamundra and, later, Kinchela homes set up as training schools. A.P.B. Inspectors had full powers

1932 The Family Endowment Department was to pay money to the A.P.B. which in turn was to spend it on food and clothing. A few cases were allowed supervised payment subject to 'investigation and report by local officers'.

The A.P.B. asked for power to concentrate on to reserves people of Aboriginal blood, to have definite control over them, and for them not to be at liberty to leave without permission

1940 Education taken over by the Education Department —qualified teachers. Separate schools to be phased out

1941 Aboriginal Welfare Board — new policy of assimilation

1950s Separate schools closing

1953 People of Aboriginal parentage to be admitted to Teachers Colleges
Children sent to homes as Wards of the State — through the Courts

1955 Separate syllabus, based on 1916, discussed — decision negative. Introduction of Certificate of Exemption from provisions of Aboriginal Protection Act: 'When an Aboriginal has attained a degree of social adjustment as to indicate that he or she is able to take his place as a responsible member of the Community'

1959 Federal pensions — old age, invalid — to be given to all except nomadic or primitive. Previously withheld from those on reserves

1963 The repeal of the ban on alcohol

1965 Managers dispensed with — Welfare Officers appointed

1967 Entry to reserves open to all

1968 The end of the Welfare Board

1

'HOW WILL THE WHITE MAN FIND HIS WAY THEN?'

My parents weren't married. If they'd been famous, I might have been called a 'love child'. But that was the last thing anyone thought to call me!

My father came from a 'good' white family, but was the odd man out, and my mother was Aboriginal or an 'Australian of Aboriginal descent', which is the latest title they give us. Well, that's two handicaps there's never been any escape from. I've known a few people who have added a third disadvantage — that I'm not only Aboriginal but an intelligent and capable woman! I don't know about that. Perhaps it does explain some things, especially the nature of my dear grandmother.

Yes, my grandmother. I have to speak about her first. She had a deep sense of faith — a Christian in the real sense, as well as knowing what it is truly like to be Aboriginal. She taught me how to survive without turning to a way of escape, such as drink. I've seen so many turn to that. She also taught me not to feel sorry for myself or have a chip on my shoulder about life or other people. She showed me that it just isn't enough being Aboriginal; you have to *know* all about being Aboriginal and go on from there. For my grandmother that meant putting into practice the Christian teaching of forgiveness and love instead of

1

meeting hatred with hatred. Oh yes, she was a remarkable woman.

I was born in a tent on the edge of Taree. My mother's people were living there. On the fringe of town, that was as close as the white people wanted them to come. Anyway, my mother used to go into town to work for my father's well-to-do family. He was her employer. Yet, well-to-do or not, I was still born out there in that tent.

I've been told that my father's wife did offer to bring me up, but my grandmother had already decided what to do for everybody. She was going to bring me up herself. That was the Aboriginal way, to be responsible for all of the family, not just your nearest. She became the single most important influence of my life, and the only real mother I ever knew.

My grandmother was half-caste herself. In those days, the old Aboriginal tribes wouldn't have anything to do with half-caste children. The Old Warrior, in some tribes, would look carefully at the colour of a baby's skin. If there was any lightness there, that baby would be killed or left to die because it was considered to be a bad omen. It would bring what we'd call today bad luck to the whole tribe.

That's what happened to her. Her mother was of the Opossum clan of the Biripi tribe. Her father was Irish. Her mother died when she was an infant and the tribe simply abandoned her because they blamed her for her mother's death. She had the lighter skin, you see. The people just left her behind when they moved camp.

Luckily a stockman found her and went after the tribe but they still wouldn't have anything to do with her. She was evil, they said. Finally the station people took her in and brought her up. She went on from there with the daughter when that lady got married, until she decided that her place was back with the Aborigines. They needed her more.

She had a couple of brothers. Their fathers were station men and they brought them up working on cattle properties and with horses. They were both big men. The elder, John, weighed about fourteen stone but I remember them saying

2

that he could ride all day and still wouldn't sweat his horse; a sign of a good horseman. The other brother, Jim, became a rough rider at shows and a horse-breaker. Both he and his wife died very young and Grandmother looked after their children.

Grandmother had the Aboriginal name of Kundaibark which meant 'The wild apple tree'. She was born under a wild apple tree, you see. As well as the Biripi tribe, she also came from the Winmurra, or 'hill country', tribes. This was the name given, especially to the women, to the tribes that came from the mountainous country in this part of the coast. Now, the Winmurra women were bigger and more heavily-built than women from the coastal tribes. They had long black hair, whereas the smaller Mariket women of the coast had short, ropey hair. The Winmurra were supposed to be very possessive about their men. The coastal men were afraid of them because not only were the Winmurra capable of taking them against their will, but they were also so very clever that they could even do the hunting! It wasn't too long ago that the young men on the coast used to joke about the Winmurra women grabbing one of their friends if he didn't watch out.

In fact, there is a local legend about an old hag, a Winmurra, who was determined to catch a husband. She came down near Forster where two men had gone up the lakes fishing. While she was waiting, she plaited a rope and put it in the water so that their canoe would snag on it. That's what happened when the two men returned. She leapt into their canoe, but they clubbed her and threw her over a cliff. There's a big rock at that place; we call it the 'Granny Rock'. That was one Winmurra who didn't get her man!

My grandmother might have been illiterate but she was a very wise and clever woman. She had learned a lot from her white foster family. When she came back to her people, she then learned the Aboriginal language so fluently that she could tell you what part of the country someone came from just by listening to the accent. By then she was more than welcome to the tribespeople. In fact, they came to trust her and to need her because, as settlement spread and fences went up, they couldn't get their food without going into paddocks. They were always being punished for stealing but if they didn't 'steal', they'd starve. There was no choice; it was just a vicious circle. They found they could turn to her and she was able to explain things and help them understand.

Then there were the diseases that were new to them and the white man's drink. Grandma could nurse them. But she would never have them inside her house. There was a lot of T.B. around then, you see. She'd give them a cup of tea, always out of tin mugs she had hanging outside. I don't know how she knew about hygiene and nursing and things like that. I suppose some doctor told her what to do. She was always very careful and made us do the right thing, too. That's probably why it used to hurt so much when people treated me as though I was one of these old tribal people. Anyway, they were white man's diseases the tribes were suffering from, when all's said and done.

I used to hear many stories about the settlers taking the law into their own hands and wiping out, not just the guilty one, but whole tribes. The word Belbowrie means 'the place of mourning' and was the name given to a place around there where a tribe was given poisoned dampers to eat. I was told about a massacre at Soldiers Point, too. The way I heard it, a man called Cromarty, a big landowner, invited a whole tribe to a feast. He poisoned the bullocks he had roasting on spits and practically the whole tribe was murdered. I was told there were skeletons being washed up on that beach long after that day. Oh yes, there were other versions and many other stories. They all told about the clash between tribal ways and the spread of what is called civilisation.

Way back, my mother's people were starting to overcrowd that camp of theirs on the fringe of the town. The problem was that the more they increased in numbers, the more the white people wanted them to keep out of town.

4

In those days, my grandfather worked a lot for the local farmers. One day he talked about the terrible conditions that they had to put up with in that camp to a Scottish couple, the McClennans. They were so sympathetic that they offered him a little corner of their own land. It was only a little square that had two entrances because different families owned the paddocks on either side of it, but it was enough for Grandfather. He returned to the camp and managed to get three or four families to move out there with him. The rest just stayed where they were. That was the year I was born, 1902.

My grandfather helped them to build their own houses from the timber around there. He even cut shingles for the roofs. He was a great shingle cutter in days when wooden shingles were used a lot. He'd worked in some of the camps in the forest for shingle cutters when he was younger. Anyway, the women had to scrub the floorboards with stones to make them smooth. This was the way it was done in those days and you can still see old houses around here that started off this way.

We had two bedrooms, a big living room and a verandah. That was considered well-off then! Later, one more room was put on the side of the verandah. There were my grandparents, their two boys and two girls, and me and we all had to live in that house. Another of their daughters was married and had a smaller house nearby. At Christmas, the whole family would come home and they'd have to use tents.

Now, Christmas we really enjoyed. Going into town to see the shops with the trees tied to the verandah posts. Buying our little gifts. Everybody happy and not much bitterness. Oh, it was fun then.

That bit of land my grandfather built on was the beginning of the settlement that came to be called Purfleet. The government set aside twelve acres and then it was increased after the managers came. Purfleet is a Scottish name and a bit odd for an Aboriginal 'village'. Actually, I did try to have it made into a real village once but I couldn't get the authorities to see eye to eye with me on that. It could so easily have developed as a proper village and perhaps things might have been different. Who knows? Just to get into town to see a doctor or go to hospital was a two mile walk. There were no buses then. You'd have to wait when you got there, too. It was the same for everyone, black or white, who couldn't afford a horse and sulky. That's why bush nurses like my grandmother were always kept busy. She'd go to the isolated houses and even stay overnight if it was too far or too late to walk back home. And when someone died at the hospital, the men had to go and borrow a hand cart from Mr McClennan so that they could wheel the body back the three-mile journey to our cemetery.

My grandfather was coastal ... and half-caste, too. He had an Aboriginal mother and a Scottish father who was drowned at sea. His father owned a lot of property but he didn't inherit any of it. All that he got was a bit of land out at Coolongolook to build a house on. I'm pretty sure that's where he met Grandmother. He was brought up by white people, too. They didn't want him to go back to the Aborigines as my grandmother wanted. But he did, even though he was always inclined more towards the white people. He got on really well with a lot of them.

You know, in those days, in many things, there wasn't much difference between us and poor white people — except for the one thing we could never escape from, the colour of our skins. It didn't help at all being half-caste, like so many of us were. In fact, as far as I'm concerned, this is our main problem in this part of Australia even today. Many of us are people who belong to two races but don't really fit in with either. I've spoken to a lot of people about this. Even young people are still feeling themselves pulled in two different directions. I guess it's much the same in many parts of the world. But our problem is made more acute because of our skin colour. I had an Irish friend who once said to me, 'Ella, you'll always be noticed because of the colour of your skin and you'll always feel you have to do things better than everyone else because of it.' I've found that to be very true.

6

This colour of our skins will disappear through inter-marriage because, unlike other dark races, there are no 'throwbacks' with the Aboriginal. It'll just disappear eventually. I told an old full-blood blacktracker this once. He thought for a while, then looked at me and said, 'How will the white man find his way then?'

2

'I WANT YOU ALWAYS TO WEAR SHOES'

I know my father's parents were early settlers. I don't know who his mother was. I think his father was English, but that's as far as I do know. He had brothers and sisters, but I'm not sure how many. One sister I particularly know about lived up at Murwillumbah in the later part of her years. I tried to get in touch with her when Dad died, but she was so very old by then. One of his brothers lived in Taree; he was well up on the council and a street is named after him. Another brother was killed on the race track but I don't know how. All I do know is that he was interested in horse racing and raced some horses.

My father married a local girl. They had five children, who all managed to get into good jobs in Sydney. They were all well-educated and had married well. I think they were ashamed to be related to me just as much for that as for the fact that I had Aboriginal blood in me.

I remember when my father died, having to face that family again.

I didn't find out who my father was until just after my grandfather died. I think Aunty Rachel was the cause. She was the one who did all the straight talking in our family, and was always wanting to get things out into the open. She was the wild one, too; she forever wanted to put us right about things or to tell us what we ought to say and do.

I must have been almost eleven when Grandfather died. I remember Aunty Rachel taking my grandmother aside and speaking to her, then Grandmother calling me over and making me sit solemnly alongside of her. She put her arms around me and said, 'I want to tell you something about this man who calls you "my girl".' What she told me after that changed my whole outlook on life.

Before this, she had refused to tell me who my father really was. My mother died young, before I could really get to know her, but at least I knew something about her by the way they talked of her. Yet my father's name had never been mentioned. I wasn't really interested anyway, if the truth be known, because as far as I was concerned Grandfather was all the father I needed.

So Grandmother and I sat there. She informed me that the white man I used to go and visit in Wingham was actually my own father. It was something I had never even dreamt of. Oh, I used to worry a bit that he called me 'my girl' and had often wondered to myself, 'Now, why does he call me that?' But this was now something quite different. When I was told it, I was terribly hurt. I don't know why. I just didn't want it that way at all. No, I couldn't accept it. I felt dreadful. It was one thing to have been visiting him, but quite another to learn that I was his child and that he was keeping me. It really rocked my boat.

Grandmother then told me that my mother had married in 1907 and died in 1909. It was said that she had caught typhoid from the paint they had used on the walls of the house. I listened, but I couldn't feel any love for her. I had never been with her, never known her as mother. Years later, I asked Dad, 'What was my mother like? I don't even remember what her face was like.'

He answered, 'Your mother was lovely. She had a lovely face. She was a lovely person, always smiling. She was a very happy person.' He went on after a while, 'There is

9

one thing about your mother. She always thought you were gold and, my word, if she could see you now she'd think you were still a lump of gold!'

That was the only time I heard him say something about my mother and me.

Grandmother wasn't finished with telling me upsetting things. She had made up her mind to explain everything, and she did. She told me the story of how I was born and how she had taken me in. Being a single girl, my mother couldn't keep me because she had to work. Later, when she got married, it was too late to take me back. The man she had married — my step father — had never settled down. He was a masterful horseman and was always away droving cattle or breaking in horses. His people came from around Wingham, but I never saw much of him either.

The bottom fell right out of my world as I sat on that seat listening to my grandmother. Looking back on it now I think it's the greatest mistake a person can do to wait until an adopted child is set in her ways before telling her the truth. It's too late to make adjustments. When someone tells you that she's not your real mother or he's not your real father, you get tormented suddenly about who you really are and what you are. You just don't know what to think. Then a kind of rebellion starts creeping into your heart and slowly but surely you begin to lose your love for the person who reared you. Oh, it's still there, of course, but you just begin to have this nagging thought, 'Well, you're not mine; you have no right to say this or that to me.'

It's not only that. It's also a tremendous shock to suddenly learn that your 'brothers' and 'sisters' are really uncles and aunts. One 'sister' who had now become an aunt seemed to delight in taunting me with it. Every time she wanted to get me crying, she would call me by my father's name. It was even worse, because she knew I hated that name if ever I hated any name! There were times when we were blackberrying together, when all of a sudden she'd become nasty and turn on me with, 'These are my black-

10

berries and you're not to touch them!' Of course I'd answer her back, and then she'd say, 'You just shut up and just remember who you are and what you are.'

Oh, that used to upset me. I'd cry out to her, 'Why wasn't I left alone. Let me remember what I remember!' But there would always be a next time.

All my life I have felt that everybody misunderstood me, especially when I was little. I always seemed to be in the road of people because I was always trying to help. Little as I was, I'd try to carry things or tidy up but I was always roused on. The only really happy times, when I felt I belonged, was when we got together at night and grandmother would make us read the Bible and she would sit and listen and talk about the things we read and we would wait for the time when she would stand. Then she would bring us right back to the old Aboriginal way of thinking and talking about the legends, about the Dreamtime. I think I enjoyed that most. I was so happy sitting there and listening to the beautiful things she told us and they were so near to the Bible stories we had just read. Then she would tell us about Coolumbra.

Coolumbra was travelling with his tribe from the Wallamba to the coast near Blackhead. He said goodbye to his mother and told her to hang up his 'bulli baun' (loin cloth made from kangaroo skin) and, when she would see blood dripping from it, she would know he had been killed. Now, Coolumbra was a very good man and so clever that the others were jealous and said they would kill him. When they got to an opening in the rocks along the seashore, they could not cross it so he told them to go around. He crossed the opening and, when the others arrived, there was Coolumbra on the beach with a fire burning and fish cooking on the coals and he also had honey for them to eat. His enemies were able to catch him there, tie him to a tree and they then speared him to death. His mother knew he was dead because blood dripped from his bulli baun as he had said.

11

I was taken to the only tree on that beach, a mangrove tree. We were told not to touch this tree. If we did, it would bring very heavy rain.

Anyway, after a while I started to think of my father as my father. I'll always remember writing my first letter to him. It was a strange feeling to start it 'Dear Dad'. I had nobody to take me to see him then and he had been after me to drop him a line. I knew how proud I had made him by starting to call him 'Dad'. That hadn't been as hard for me as I thought it would have been, so I decided to write the letter. It seems a trifling thing now but it was a big step for me then. I suppose I was just beginning to realise that he was the only thing I had then. Grandfather had gone and Grandmother's life seemed to be changing. It might have been me after our talk together, but somehow she seemed to be getting further away from me.

In fact, everything wasn't the same any more. I just couldn't get used to calling anything different the people I had always thought of as being my brothers and sisters. It was so hard to say 'uncle' or 'aunt' when I'd been using Bill, Arthur, Elsie and Mabel all my life. On the other hand I was now their niece and it didn't seem right calling them by their first names either. Somehow, the more I told myself that I would have to adjust, the harder it became to adjust.

When people asked me what my name was and I'd answer that it was Russell, back would come the reply, 'How come? That's your mother's name.' Nobody had questioned it before, but now they did. Oh, it was all right when I was under the security of having Grandfather, but now they wanted to draw me out on why I refused to change my name. I didn't see why I had to use a different name after all these years. I suppose it's the same for all adopted children when they're told, but it used to upset me so. I wasn't ashamed of being a Russell and, anyway, I just couldn't bring myself to like my father's name. I won't disclose what it was, because of his relatives and because I loved my father.

12

My father told me later that it was a party at his place that led to my being born. As I said, my mother was actually working for him at the time. He was always very sorry that I had come into life that way.

His wife was very understanding about it, or so he said. If it hadn't been for my grandmother I might well have been brought up as a white. But that doesn't mean to say that I was accepted by the Aborigines, either. Well, I was more than half white, so where was I, half white and half black, supposed to go? Where was I supposed to fit in?

It's funny how the ones who wouldn't accept me as Aboriginal seemed to care even less about the language than I did. Wherever I went in New South Wales I wanted to know about the tribal ways, wanted to hear the languages. I wanted to teach our language to the young ones even though they'd tell me, 'Oh, don't give us that! We can't talk like that. Nobody talks like that any more.' One of my own grandsons said that to me. I knew more about our common Aboriginal heritage than they did — so who was white and who was black?

I could never understand why they seemed to be ashamed of it. The more I have learned about the part of me that is Aboriginal the prouder I have become. Nowadays I find myself being almost the only one left who knows the local language — some use a few words but, more often than not, they're not even words from this area; it's another language. Even some of the legends they tell are not ours.

My father was a saddler by trade. He was very clever at it, too, and used to make some beautiful saddles. Oh yes, he often won prizes for them. I remember he worked for an old fellow who owned a shop in Taree and he'd do all the repairing of saddles and things.

Then he owned his own shop up at Wingham. That was when I was only a tiny tot. One of my aunts used to take me up there to visit him and there I'd be, wondering why I had to go so far to see this old man who meant nothing to me then.

You know, I always remember my Dad with a shock of white hair and moustache. I never saw him without white hair. When I got older and was beginning to muster up the courage to ask him personal things, I asked him why he had white hair all the time. He said, 'In the early days I had an operation between the eyes. Something happened there. Now, there's this sort of "sympathy cord" between your two eyes and as soon as one eye gets hurt, the other eye cries and they have to cut the "sympathy cord". After that, my hair went white!' I was never sure whether he was joking.

My father was always kind to me, too. He gave me money when I needed it, and bought what things he could for me. Though I never fully understood it, I never questioned that, I can tell you! But, even though I was still a child, I used to occasionally wonder why. One day, he turned to me suddenly and said, 'I want you always to wear shoes.'

I'll never forget that. He was as good as his word, too. I was never without a good pair of shoes. Being a saddler, of course, he could not only mend them, but make them, as well. Right up until I got married, I'd never throw away a pair no matter how worn out they were. I knew he'd do them up, when I saw him again. In fact, I hardly ever had to buy a pair of shoes. When he made them, they were such really good leather shoes that I never had the trouble other children had. I would even run about in the wet weather with them on.

Talking of shoes, there was one day I will never forget. It was the day of the opening of the Taree Railway Station. I had this new pair of shoes, but they were so hard that I could hardly walk in them. One of my aunts was going to the opening and she said, 'Look, you get used to those shoes and you can come with me.' I was delighted. I was going to get used to them in time, or bust. So I put them on, laced them up, and ran down the hill to the creek. I ran and ran through all the great big puddles down there, so that they would stretch and fit my feet, you see. Oh, I wanted so much to go to that opening, I didn't care about getting my feet soaking wet, just as long as I could go.

Finally I ran back up the hill and arrived back home. By this time, those shoes were just beautifully worn in; all I had to do was change my socks and I'd be ready to go with her. But when I got inside, I found that she'd already left. I was so disappointed that I just sat down. I never did see that first train come in. All that trouble for nothing! Oh, I can laugh about it now. What made it even worse then was that it took me days to dry my shoes out again. At least they fitted me after that.

Yes, I often wondered why I had to go so much to see this old man in Wingham. I didn't have to go every week and I used to stay with an aunt I had who lived there with her family. She had a daughter called Zillah May, and I used to go to school there with her whenever I was visiting. But sooner or later my grandmother would send word that it was time for me to come home again. For some reason, she never let me stay away for very long. So no more school there until I came up next time. It was all a bit odd, I admit, but not as odd as this white-haired man, who I would never have thought could be my father. He would always greet me with a, 'How are you, my girl?' and I would think, 'Well, I'm not your girl', but I never said anything.

I used to watch him work. I remember when it was a bit cold, he'd give me a piece of that material that he used to line the saddles with. It was high quality cloth and it'd make a splendid blanket for us. I can still see him bringing up this piece of blanket, if he'd forgotten to give it to me. It kept me warm when I was staying with Zillah May and my aunt, at least. I had to stay there overnight, even if I wanted to return the same day. The trains were difficult then. They would go up in the morning and they wouldn't come back to Taree until too late in the evening.

When my father died, I had to find the place where he'd told me his own people were buried. His own family couldn't, or didn't want to, help me. All I knew was that it was an old cemetery that had been closed down. Finally, the undertaker had it opened for me and we buried him alongside of his parents and one of his brothers. By that time I was a married woman and mature, but I think his death was one of the saddest things of my life. I had accepted him and he was a good-natured man. In all that time we never quarrelled or had a cross word. He was always kind. He was always considerate.

3

'THAT OLD MAN IS MY FATHER'

He had come to live with my husband and me earlier. I still lived at Purfleet, but not on the reserve. It didn't matter whether I did or not; as far as most people thought, if you lived at Purfleet, you lived on the reserve. There was no distinction. Anyway, my father was there with us. But, you see, we had Aboriginal blood, so his family got upset about it.

They said it wasn't right, and they got the manager of the reserve onto us. Even though we weren't living on that reserve, my father had to walk through the reserve to get to our house and so the manager still thought they could enforce the law that a white man wasn't supposed to live with Aborigines on the reserve. The Protection Board, as it was called then, had brought that one in. No, my own father couldn't stay with me, the manager said, as long as we lived anywhere on Purfleet. He even admitted that if I hadn't lived on Purfleet, the Board wouldn't have had the power to do this and would have left him alone.

Oh, there was such a down on Purfleet in those days. If anyone came from Purfleet, they were 'black' and that was it. Even the white missionaries who came there to live used to be called 'black'. They were thought of as being even worse precisely because they volunteered to live there.

17

This sort of prejudice went on for years. It's only been in recent years that this sort of thing has broken down somewhat. I remember when people used to even follow other white people visiting friends on the reserve and shout insults and things at them. There used to be a lot of fights then, I can tell you. The silly thing is that there are now just as many white people as black people living on the place, because there's been so much intermarriage over the years. They marry and they stay there. It's not so much of a 'black's camp' now.

So it was too 'degrading' for my father's family to think that they had one of their own kind living with me, and on Purfleet of all places. Anyway, after that manager had spoken to me, I went back and spoke to my father about it. He didn't know what to do. It was just like being thrown out of your own home. The only place he could think of going to was one of his old friends' places down on one of the islands. There was no alternative. He had to leave us, so he went and lived down there. But he used to come back to town often and we'd meet, and at Christmas time he would still come out to Forster with us to stay for the holidays.

My father's brother was Town Clerk. That's how they were able to make so much fuss about his staying with me. Oh, it wasn't fuss that was out in the open, though. They managed to keep it very quiet, in fact. What could I say? Even after my father had died, they wanted to keep it under their hats, that he had ever lived with me. I only found out later that his niece — she owned a boarding house in the town — had asked a friend of my mother what sort of person I was. That friend used to work for her at the boarding house. So they were interested enough to find out what I was like. Anyway, my mother's friend told her I was a nice person. But then she went on to say that I lived out at Purfleet, and that was enough said as far as she and the rest of my father's family were concerned. They were so much against anybody who lived at Purfleet.

18

One day, my father, my husband and I were on the bus, going out to Forster during our holidays. There was an old man who used to live around about Stoney Creek. Actually, I'd known him since I was a child, because he used to often give us a ride from the town. As we got off the bus, my husband naturally got off and helped my father down.

This old man from Stoney Creek came up to me soon after and said, 'You know, I've been watching your husband and how kindly he treats that old man.'

I said, 'That old man is my father.'

It didn't seem to shock him at all. All he did was to reply, 'I was just watching how kindly he treated him. He got off the bus and put his arm out and then put him down so gently. It really touched me. It's good to know there's still some kindness left in the world.' My father was in his eighties by then.

It wasn't so long after that that we began to get the orders that he must leave us. I knew he needed somebody and that nobody else wanted him. He was old. He was a sick old man. But I couldn't do anything. They just wouldn't let him alone.

Not very long after he had left me, my father fell ill and, of course, I didn't know about it. The first I heard of it was when one of the Purfleet women came to me and said she'd read a piece in the paper about him being taken off to hospital as an emergency case. She'd seen him around the settlement when he was staying with me. They all liked him and knew he was my father. It was all right for her to tell me I ought to go and see him, but what if I went and visited him and they didn't believe I was his daughter? What then?

Oh, I was in a state when I went to work that morning. I didn't know what to do. It was horrible. I was dreadfully worried about him, but I was also fearful that if I went to the hospital, they might say, 'Oh no, that can't be your father. He's a white man.' Or something like that.

At that time I was working for a couple named Patterson who were teachers. I went around working in their house all that morning, trying to work up the nerve to tell her why I wanted to go to the hospital. I just didn't know what reaction I would get. I just worked on until I couldn't stand it any longer. I forced myself to go up to Mrs Patterson and managed to get out, 'There is something I want to say!' I must have said it pretty urgently, because she looked at me in surprise and asked me what was wrong.

Then I opened my heart to her. I told her my father was in hospital and he was a white man. I said I wanted desperately to go and visit him but was afraid to because there were only a few people who actually knew he was my father.

Well, Mrs Patterson and I had known each other for some time by then, and we respected each other. She used to teach me how to arrange flowers and I'd not only do the work around the house, but go shopping for her as well. I think she was more startled that I could be afraid of anything. What really worried me in particular was having to go to the Matron there to ask where my Dad was. Black people just didn't go and visit white people in hospital then, let alone advertise that an old white man was their father.

Fortunately, Mrs Patterson fixed it all up. She got on the telephone and called the Matron of the hospital. I heard her say over the phone that she was sending 'her girl' up who wanted to see her Dad and that she'd appreciate it if the Matron was kind to me. And off I went. I still wasn't all that happy about it, but at least I knew that if Matron got nasty, she would have to face Mrs Patterson after having promised to look after me. That thought gave me more courage and I quite looked forward to visiting my father.

When I got to the hospital, I found the Matron's office and asked where my father was. I gave her his name. She looked up at me and then told me that he had died. Just like that. Oh, my father had died, and I wasn't there by his side . . .

They didn't even know who his family was or who they should have contacted. In the meantime he had been put down in the Morgue. She asked me to identify him, because he had died on the Wednesday before and it was already near the end of the week. What could I say? I didn't want to see him like that, but I had to say I would.

One of the nurses took me down to the Morgue. I felt so sad and terrible. It was the first time I had been in a Morgue and it was the first time I'd ever seen how they put the bodies in a sort of ice box. How could my own father end up in a place like this? They pulled a body out. There was his lovely white moustache. I said, 'Yes, that's my father.'

At the hospital they also asked me about the funeral arrangements. How would I know? Where was the rest of his family? None of them had been near him.

So I said that I would make them, if I possibly could. I had to. I was the only member of the family there. So I went down and spoke to the undertaker about it. The first thing he wanted to know was where Dad was to be buried. Luckily, my father had confided in me about who his parents were and where they'd been buried, so I told the undertaker about the old cemetery.

I've already told you how we had to go out there and unlock it. It was so old and disused. We found the spot and he marked it out; it was right next to my father's parents and one of his brothers.

Anyway we arranged that my father would be buried on a certain day at eleven o'clock in the morning. A feeling of being pleased that I was being useful at last came over me. It wasn't until I got back home that night that grief suddenly hit me. He had passed away with nobody by his side after all those years of being kind to me. I hadn't even been able to return that kindness in his last days when he really needed somebody. He had always been such a lonely old fellow. It was terrible he had to die so lonely as well.

21

By the time the day had come for the funeral, I had finished a nice little wreath. The missionary at the settlement had agreed to take me into town to the undertaker in his car. We arrived there right on eleven o'clock, the time it was due to start.

But there was no evidence of a funeral about to start. I found the undertaker around the back and asked him why. He said, 'I'm terribly sorry, but I had word from the family. They said they were coming up from Sydney and wouldn't get in until four o'clock. They said they would pay all the expenses for the funeral too . . . on one condition.' He hesitated then, and I demanded to know what condition. 'That you stay away, Ella!'

I almost cried out, 'But I'll only be standing there looking and I'm going with the missionary. Who's going to know I'm related?'

The undertaker sat there for a while, then said softly, 'They will, Ella. Look, they're going to pay. They've got the money. His nephew owns racehorses. So why don't you just let them pay?'

I said, 'I'll pay for the funeral, then!'

He shook his head. 'Ella,' he said, 'they've got more money than you. I won't let you pay out all this money. Look, if you want, I'll take you out to see the grave now . . . anything, to make it up to you.'

How could that make it up to me? I think that's the very first time I felt so desperately angry about prejudice that I was going to dig my toes in and fight. I just couldn't take this. He was my father, too. I was going to go whether they liked it or not.

I went back out to the car and told the missionary what had happened. I was so furious. He cooled me down a bit and started to talk about it — that I had done everything I could for my father when he was alive and again at the hospital, but this wasn't going to be any use to him at all now. All it was going to do was to get myself hurt.

He was right, of course. Once I became more collected, I could see that. I didn't stay on there and I didn't come back for the funeral later that day. I only turned to the

22

missionary and said, 'I've been hurt so much and for so long, I suppose this doesn't matter. I'll go home, thank you.'

One of the greatest trials of my life was to try to forgive these people for that. They had nothing to do with my father when he was living. And there I was, so much in his life over those last few years, and yet I wasn't deemed good enough to be allowed to go to his funeral. I had looked after him as best I could. I had told the authorities where to find these people so they could be notified of his death. I had shown the place where he had wanted to be buried. And more than all of that, I loved him; he was my father. It didn't make the slightest difference to them. I couldn't even stand by and just watch. I was still a secret that had to be kept from the world — something that was shameful, something whose very existence was distasteful.

I was so angry still that my first impulse was to let the cat out of the bag about it. But then it came back to me how my grandmother had drummed it into me that God made all people equal; colour is only skin deep and that the strong thing was to return forgiveness to those who hurt you. It took me a long time, I can tell you, but finally I did it. I can truly say that, with God's help, I have forgiven them a long time ago.

Anyway, I went back home with the missionary and tried to pretend that I wasn't hurt by what had happened. I tried my best not to show that the first thing I really wanted to do was just to cry. But when we were walking around the back of the mission home, I'm afraid it hit me too hard. I am not a crier, but, oh, I cried then. I just sobbed and sobbed. After all those years, my father . . .

The missionary wasn't expecting this; all he could do was to pat me on the back and say, 'Don't cry, please don't cry.' He couldn't know that after all those years it wasn't right that my father and I should end like that.

I was so sad in my heart for so long that I thought it was going to burst. All of us — my husband, my children and myself — felt a deep sense of grief for a long time. Each of us had grown to love him. He had been such a grand old fellow.

Soon after that I went back to pick up some things my father had promised me. He had left them with an old man who used to work with him. I didn't know what I could tell him, so all I said was that I had come about some things left by the man he used to work with. He looked at me, then straight away, said, 'You wouldn't be Sam's daughter, would you?' I told him, yes, I was. Then he went on, 'You know, Sam spoke of you for many years. The things he said about you were very, very good. I often used to ask Sam why he didn't forget about you and he'd say, "No, I couldn't do that. I couldn't let her go." He was really fond of you. I'm glad I've met you after all these years. Now I know what sort of person you are.'

I never saw that friend of my father again. He was living at the boarding house that belonged to my father's niece. I'm sure she was the one who started all the fuss about me going to the funeral. Anyway, that friend of my mother — the one who worked there — told me later that he had gone straight back to the boarding house and told this niece that he had just met a 'relation' of hers. I don't know if he did that because he was on my side and was enjoying having a dig at her, or whether he was trying to show some sort of sympathy with her for having me as a cousin. He might have been boasting to her that he had found out her secret. I wouldn't know. I wouldn't even know if he even disliked the idea of his friend Sam having a part-Aboriginal as a daughter. It doesn't matter. The thing is that I never heard from that niece again. So it had a purpose at least.

Then there was one of my father's brothers who I used to often see when I was in town at the Post Office. When I was getting the mail for the people I was working for, I'd nearly always run into this little old fellow buying a paper. He'd always be looking me up and down out of the corner of his eye. I used to wish I could read his thoughts. I mean, was there ever just a little doubt in his mind about the family dismissing me out of hand? Did he ever wonder what I was really like? Did he ever think that my father might not have done something so dreadfully bad in conceiving me as they had made out he had? If he did, he never said a word. I didn't speak to him either. I never gave him a chance.

You know, I was never given any of my father's things, except the bits that old fellow had, even those that he had promised to me. No, that's wrong. Up at the hospital, they gave me his pyjamas!

I've been asked if the same thing happened now, would I do the same things all over again. I don't think it would ever arise today. The attitudes of people are so different, thank God. I think all this publicity about racial prejudice and prejudice against illegitimates too has helped to bring things out into the open more. Yet I suppose somebody had to suffer at first, so that we could all know how people who have to suffer such things feel, and how we should treat all people with respect. We had to learn the hard way before we knew what to do and what needed to be done.

All I know is that I'd put up more of a fight today. Oh yes, I'd be having a real go. There'd be a few of them who'd get a telling off, I can tell you.

4

'THE DEVIL TOLD
ME TO!'

One of my very first memories was being on holidays with a close girl friend of mine. For some reason her nickname was always George. On this day I am thinking about George and I were sitting right in the middle of a paddock. The weeds were so high that they reached well over our heads. She turned to me and said, 'Let's have a smoke!'

Now, I'd always been told it was dreadfully wrong for girls to smoke cigarettes, but she picked up a hollow stem there and lit it with a match she had. Then she began to draw on it and blow it out just as though she was smoking a real cigarette. Well, it was real enough for us then.

She took a few puffs, then offered it to me. I was dying to know what it was like, so it didn't take much urging from George to get me to have a go at it. So I took it and had a 'smoke' too.

At home that night, a woman I didn't know at all well took me aside and asked me, 'Were you smoking with George today?' Of course, I wanted to hotly deny it, and nearly did. But I could hear Grandmother's voice always telling me that I must tell the truth no matter what. Besides, I must have sensed I looked guilty as I could be, so I confessed that I had been. As I did so, I was just hoping that this woman wouldn't tell my family.

Then she asked me who had told me to smoke. Now, I didn't want to get George into trouble on my account, so I replied as quick as a wink, 'The Devil told me to!'

This curious woman didn't bat an eyelid at my saying that. She just smiled a bit and asked me, 'Well, which hand did the Devil make you hold the smoke in?' When I told her, she took hold of that offending hand, turned it over until my palm was facing upwards, and then slapped it good and hard. When she had finished she told me not to smoke ever again.

I'm not telling you this because of the slapping. In fact, I didn't mind that at all. I remember lying in bed that night, feeling all the better for it. I had been purged of all the wrong things I had done that day, so I didn't have a bad conscience, I suppose.

No, I'm telling you this because I later found out that this strange woman was, in fact, my real mother. Her name was Lucy Ann, and this is the first memory I have of her, knowing that she was my real mother. Before I hadn't noticed her much.

There were times when I longed for my mother, especially during the time I was a teenager. I loved Grandmother, of course, but whenever I turned to her, say, when I had been hurt or was having one of those puppy love affairs that so upset teenagers, she'd only say that God knew all about these things so I'd better ask Him. Now that was fine, but it didn't help much for what I wanted to find out then. I felt that if I could just talk to my real mother, then she would understand and would explain how I could get over these growing pains of one thing or another. Like every other child, things just came crowding in on me in those days.

My Grandmother's way of commending me to God's love and understanding did at least take much of the violence out of me. I could get really angry for my age and, being a big girl, wouldn't think twice about belting up any of the kids who dared to make me angry.

I wasn't always on the winning side, though. I remember when I was little we had a paling fence around our place and the gate used to slam shut. It always seemed to be shut when it should be open. Anyway, this day I trotted after the big girls when they went out to play. As usual, they got into a quarrel with one particular girl and the inevitable fight started. I was still too young to join in, but I waited my chance to have a go and then jumped in and gave her a hard thump right on the back. She turned around to go for me, of course. I took off for home, running as fast as my little legs would go, with this girl hard on my heels. I managed to beat her to my place, but when I went to throw myself into the safety of my own front yard, I found that that gate had gone and shut itself again. And I was much too small to open it myself. That big girl trapped me and gave me a good belting in return. I never tried anything like that again, unless I knew for sure that that gate was open. If I couldn't win, I didn't want to be in it!

When the railway was being built, there were workers' tents everywhere. I still remember seeing them in what was then bush around the Dawson River.

Some of my uncles were working on the project and my aunts and uncles used to take us to spend the weekend down there. This gave my grandmother a break from all the kids. Being children, of course, we used to lag behind on the way there, poking our noses into everything and being general busybodies.

I remember this time we'd reached the last bit of bush before the camp. Lo and behold, we saw a koala sleeping in a branch of a tree. It was just there minding its own business, but, no, I just had to climb that tree and hand him down to the others. Now that bear just sat there sleeping away. How it let me handle it, I'll never know! But it did.

I had my usual pinafore on. They were pretty common in those days. Most girls ran around in them to save their clothes. I needed one especially. I always seemed to get so dirty or tear my dresses. I'd be forever coming home from school with bits of material hanging from the frills and ruffles of my dresses.

Anyway, there I was, up the tree with that koala. I put my pinny over its head and tied it on its back so it wouldn't slip off. Then I handed it down to the other three children I was with. It never batted an eyelid. It didn't struggle or anything; not a murmur. It even seemed to like us. Oh, I thought it was lovely; I thought that I had found my pet for life at last.

I jumped down from the tree and somehow got hold of one of its 'hands'. Then the whole five of us carried on following my aunts and uncles. Would you believe it, that bear just walked quietly between us with my pinny still tied around its head!

We were almost up to the tents, when suddenly the koala began to fight back furiously. They've got claws when they want to use them, too! I guess it must have just woken up, or something. What followed then was a mad struggle, with the bear trying to get back to the bush and me trying to rescue my pinny without getting scratched. Somehow, both it and I succeeded. It got its bush and I got my pinny, and I had nothing more to show for it than a few scratches on my arms. You should have seen that koala move!

When one of my aunts found out what we'd been doing, she thought we were mad. She told us never to go near animals in the bush that were asleep or just minding their own business. I didn't need to be told a second time!

Once there was really heavy rain and the creek down on the flat flooded. Of course, the first thing we kids wanted to do was to go down and see the floodwaters. We got down there and started a game of chasings. I was 'he'. I was chasing a couple of them and was just about to catch them when they jumped over one part. I just took off too, forgetting that I was much shorter than they. I landed right in the middle of it. I've never got such a shock! When I got home, I was still soaking wet.

I remember that because it just seems to me that I was always getting into trouble one way or another.

Grandmother had a splendid quince stick that she put away to use on us when we got very naughty. If we were late in coming inside and heard her calling us, we'd dash into the house and dive under the bed to get away from that quince stick. One of my aunts once dived under it so blindly that she nearly cut off her finger on Grandfather's best axe. My grandmother immediately forgot about us, of course, and looked after the finger. Oh, we were all very sorry it had happened, but we were secretly very pleased. If it hadn't happened, we would have got a dose of that quince stick.

You know, there was a lot of millet and corn growing around Taree when I was a child. The men used to get a lot of work out of corn pulling and millet cutting. Their families used to work alongside of them too.

They used to 'table' the millet. That meant that you broke the millet behind you and put the 'tables' across a bench. You'd be in one row doing this and somebody else would be in the next row doing it the other way. That meant you could stand looking along between each pair of rows and see one big line of millet heads going this way and that way. We children were fascinated by seeing that pattern once the 'tables' had been tapered level. Then a man would come down through the middle of the rows and with a sharp blade cut the tops this side, that side, this side, that side, and so on.

Oh, there was certainly no shortage of millet cutters then. They'd use the ends of the millet to make brooms in the broom factory at Tinonee. That was another source of employment.

The money mightn't have seemed much out in the fields in those days, but things were so cheap and wages went quite a long way. The Aborigines didn't need welfare then; they made their own money. It was better.

They used to work from sunrise to sunset, too. There

wasn't any time off. If you got there early you'd get a lot of cutting work; if not, you got less. And then if it had been dewy in the morning, they didn't start cutting until the crop had dried out. You had to grab the work when it was there.

You couldn't even rely on the length of the millet season. It could vary so much. It wasn't only if it was dewy in the mornings; if the weather was wet, for example, or if the crop hadn't grown very much, the season could be very short. It was the same with the corn.

In the winter, the men used mainly to snare possums and sell the skins in a shop up at Tinonee. The skins would then be sent on to Sydney by boat.

We always loved a day off school because Grandfather wanted us to help him pull the corn. They used to pull it by hand and then stack it on a cart to go up to the barn. There, we'd all chip in and help throw all the corn into the barn. Oh, it was great fun. There we'd be, up on the cart and throwing those large cobs of corn into that barn.

We used to help him husk them too. Grandfather used to take us down at night to do this. I wasn't supposed to go because I was still too small but I always did. Wherever my grandfather went I insisted on going too. I loved him so much that he couldn't even move without me. Wherever he was I'd always be somewhere around the place.

Anyway, to start the husking off, he used to make a little sharp stick which he would put into the corn. Then you just husked it and threw the corn into a heap.

They had an old threshing machine there, but it wasn't like the type they use today. This was one that you had to turn by hand. I remember one of my aunts got on the old machine one day and one of those weevils that get into corn got into her ear. They had a terrible time getting it out again.

I said I'd always go along, but that doesn't mean to say I stayed in the barn for too long. I was too much of a busybody for that! Sooner or later I'd always end up at the farm house, gathering eggs for the old ladies there or climbing trees to get walnuts for them. Actually I got very friendly with one of those old ladies. In fact she even wanted

31

to adopt me. That wasn't possible, of course. Nevertheless, when I'd return from the farm house, the others used to tease me with, 'If you go in there with her, she'll dress you up in those old farm boots!' Oh, didn't they have great fun teasing me!

The special thing for me was listening to my grandmother talk to a kind of bird she called 'Goorie Dookie'. She called it that because of the call it had.

You know, the Aborigines used to learn a lot from birds. If there was any new kind of fruit, they'd watch to see if the birds ate it; that way they'd know if it was poisonous. Take the Willie Wagtail, too. If it was jumping about a lot and getting excited, the Aborigines would start looking around for a snake. They used to believe that it was warning them to be careful where they were walking.

Anyway, Grandmother's 'Goorie Dookie' bird is a shy, grey thing that peeps around trees and is easily frightened away by any sort of noise. It is usually with the whipbird whose call, just like a whip cracking, comes first. Now we used to wash the clothes down in a waterhole and Grandmother would take each of us girls in turn to help her do it. As soon as she heard her 'Goorie Dookie' bird, we'd have to keep very quiet while she listened to what it had to say and then talk back to it in the Biripi language.

One day when I was with her, it called its 'Goorie Dookie' three times straight and then got very excited. Gran nodded and then told me that that meant there was a person close by. Sure enough, through the bush came an Aboriginal with an axe over his shoulder.

There was another day when the 'Goorie Dookie' bird visited us again. This time it called, 'Wirrilan, wirrilan, Goorie Dookie, wirrilan.' When I asked Grandmother what that meant, she said it meant that somebody had died. The word for corpse in the local language is 'wirrilan', you see. Anyway, then she asked the bird where. The reply was 'Yer-ook' which means North. I can remember this so well, because it wasn't even a half an hour later that

32

one of my aunts called out from the top of the hill that an old lady we had known had just died up at the hospital. She used to sometimes stay with us for a while and do a bit of washing or help when things were busy. My grandmother used to have a lot of the Aborigines come to her for help and, if they were sick, she'd let them stay. Grandfather would even build them little places to rest in, because they liked their own camps, rather than the house.

So this poor old lady had died, just as my grandmother's 'Goorie Dookie' bird had told her.

We were always being told to listen to the birds whenever we went into the bush, because they could warn us of danger, or show us where water was, or just talk to us. But we had to be quiet enough to hear them. It was a lovely way of learning about the bush, listening to the birds.

Years later, after I'd worked in Sydney, I was living on a farm near Gosford. There was a lot of scrub around there, and one day I was out with my own boys. Suddenly I heard one of my grandmother's 'Goorie Dookie' birds calling. I stopped and shushed the children, telling them, 'You just sit down and we'll listen to what the bird has to say.' They were the exact words that Grandmother used to say to me.

So we listened, then the bird started up its 'Goorie Dookie' again and I told them that it was saying to us that someone was going to visit us. Of course, they just laughed at me and said I was just making it all up. But when we got back home, sure enough, sitting on the verandah, was the visitor. It was my cousin who had been in the army. He had come down with his wife to work on the farm for a while. That really showed my children!

Well, of course, they became very interested in listening to birds after that, I can tell you! They took a while to pick up the different types of bird calls, but then they were like most young ones of today — the language was no earthly use to them so why bother to learn it? I know there's a lot of young people trying to bring back some of the old ways now, and good on them. But I do wish they didn't get so mixed up, if not just plain wrong.

You rarely hear my grandmother's 'Goorie Dookie' bird nowadays. The bush is so rapidly diminishing that they're no longer around very much. They were always a very shy kind of bird.

I tried to find out the proper name of the 'Goorie Dookie' bird recently, but most of the old people who might have known it around here have died. Finally, I went into the Australian Museum when I was down in Sydney and was shown into the offices through the back where I met an expert on bird sounds. We found it. It was a Grey Thrush. He didn't in the least find it strange when I talked about my grandmother 'talking' to this bird and listening to what it had to say. He said he had studied in America where they know that the same kind of bird speaks a different 'language' in different parts of the country.

So, perhaps, the old Aboriginal ways are not so strange after all.

When she was only a tiny tot herself, my mother had a really odd pet, so the story goes. By the time anybody found out about it, it was nearly too late.

It happened because Grandmother was very methodical and always had little routine chores that her children had to do. One of these that my mother had to do was to go out and fill the water can from the dam that was nearby. They didn't have rain tanks in those days, you see. So after they had finished their meals, Grandmother would send my mother out to the dam with the can. She'd give her a bit of bread to keep her company on the way.

Well, what with Grandmother being so busy feeding the baby at this time, she didn't take much notice of how long my mother was away filling the water can. Like all children, my mother knew this and would take her time. They found out she used to play with this pet of hers before she'd turn around and come home with the water.

Anyway, this day, she came back crying her eyes out. Grandmother asked her what was wrong with her. My mother told her that her friend, Dandy, had bitten her.

'Who's Dandy? my grandmother demanded. Oh, Dandy was just her playmate. 'So where did he bite you?'

'He bit me on the foot.'

'Well, let's have a look at it,' Grandmother said and had a look at my mother's foot. There were two puncture marks. A snake's bite! Grandmother panicked so much that she dashed out of the house shouting for help.

Now there was an Aboriginal fellow outside at the time — a full blood who was a brother of a friend of my family. Gran shouted to him to come over, then pleaded with him to come inside and have a look at her little girl's foot.

He didn't hesitate, but hurried in after her. He took one look at that foot, scarified it with a bit of sharp stone they used to use to do that sort of thing, and then sucked away at it to draw out the poison. They knew he didn't have any decaying teeth or he might have been poisoned himself into the bargain. He just sucked and then spat the blood out.

Anyway, after that, Grandmother had come to her senses a bit more. She put ammonia on the wound and then went and got Grandfather. When he saw what had happened, he saddled up the horse and fairly flew down to Nabiac with my mother perched up in front of the saddle horn. The doctor there had a look at it and said that it was just as well that that man had sucked out the poison, otherwise nobody could know what might have happened.

Still, he treated my mother with an antidote and told my grandfather to get her back home as quickly as possible, but not to let her go to sleep for a while. By then, though, it was getting dark. Not only did my grandfather have to keep holding my mother so she wouldn't fall asleep, but he had to guide the horse home in the pitch dark *and* get there as soon as possible. There were no such things as roads to allow you to know exactly where you were or what direction you were going in.

How he got back so quickly, nobody knew.

He was a remarkable man with his children, my grandfather was. He even stayed up with her all night to make sure she didn't fall asleep and then in the morning, when the danger had passed, went straight out to the dam to make short work of 'Dandy'. My mother pleaded with him not to hurt Dandy — he didn't mean to bite her, she had trodden on him! But he went out looking for it just the same.

She needn't have worried, because he never found that snake. He searched and searched that place without any luck.

Dandy was a black snake. I wonder how many children would play with black snakes today?

There were still some very old tribal women living out in the bush when I was a little girl. They were the last of the Worimi tribe.

I remember one who was called Mary and another who was called Dilpre. They were so old and they had so many dogs! When I first saw them I was very frightened by them, because they were the first real full-blood Aborigines I'd ever seen who were still living in the wild. The missionaries were very kind to them and occasionally would take our Sunday School to visit them. We used to sing hymns to them. The missionary would go ahead and dress them because *we* were so afraid of going there!

Those early missionaries were brave as well as kind. Getting up here in 1902 took longer than it takes to go to Perth now. They had to come from Sydney by sea and many ships were wrecked or stranded crossing the bar at the river mouth. The first one, Miss Oldrey, married and settled up here and I often used to talk to her later on. She said she was often asked if she felt safe living among the Aborigines and, in fact, the Board wasn't happy about missionaries being on their own on a Mission. But, she said she felt safer living among the Aborigines than with her own people. When she was coming back from town there would always be about four of the men there to escort her back to the Mission — to protect her from the whites!

36

And, at night, she felt perfectly safe because she'd only have to make a slight noise and someone would pop up or call out, 'You all right, Miss Oldrey?' She said they were such kind people and so considerate, they wouldn't see you in need of food or anything like that without trying to help.

The corkwood tree grows wild on the central coast. Nowadays they extract something from it for the drug industry and send it overseas. I don't know what it is; it doesn't matter. The men around here get a bit of money by going out and collecting its leaves. Now, that tree is very poisonous, and I found that out the hard way . . .

I was having a game of ride-a-cock-horse using sticks from one of these trees when I was too young to know better. I must have imagined I was the horse, because I peeled some of the bark off with my teeth. Suddenly, Grandfather grabbed me up in his arms and ran the two miles down the lane to the river to get the punt over to the doctor's place. He thought he was never going to make it.

Well, I'm glad to say he did! Dr Gormley gave me a dose of something to force the poison up out of my stomach. It certainly worked! That was enough punishment in itself. I didn't need all those repeated reminders my grandfather gave me when he was taking me back home about never doing that again with corkwood trees because they were very, very poisonous.

As soon as he got me home all in one healthy piece he started cutting down all those trees that were growing near our place, just in case. That was just like him. He would teach us, but would never leave anything to chance once it had happened.

Talking about Dr Gormley, he had the very first motor car in the whole district. My, it was a fine thing to see! We used to hear it coming for miles away and would rush out just to have a look at it. There we'd be, lined up and waving as he went by.

37

You know, at the old punt wharf there was a butter factory. We could go over there and buy a whole pat of butter for a shilling. They just used to scoop it out of an old vat. What a treat that was!

I remember a Mr McCauley ran that factory. There's no doubt that it was a flourishing business then. There's not a sign of it left now. That's awfully sad. There was also a Mr Jim Carter who had the shop just up from the punt. We'd walk all the way there just to buy four lollies for a penny.

Mr Carter had a pet magpie. We all loved that magpie. It used to talk away like mad. We even taught it a few words of the language. Two of those words, I remember, were 'biyella kittis', which together mean 'to rouse' or 'be angry'.

Anyway, one day that poor old magpie got in the way of a man using a mower. I've got no idea how, but it did. The poor old thing's legs were cut off. It lay on the ground saying 'biyella kittis, biyella kittis'. It sounded funny at the time, but, oh, how we missed our old magpie friend!

5

'I WANT TO GO BACK TO SCHOOL'

Even at school I was never accepted as Aboriginal. They could see by my lighter skin that I was different to them. I had red hair and a freckled face.

That might be why some of my teachers and I were so close. And that didn't help to increase my popularity either! You know, I couldn't understand why I wasn't one thing or another. Whenever I went outside to play with some kiddies, there'd always be somebody there who came along and told me to get out of it and go back to where I belonged. I never knew where 'belong' meant, and neither did they, I suppose. They were just acting like all human beings do.

Some of them were very black and they'd try to get at me by saying I should have been over at Taree, at the whites' school. They would so often give me such a terrible time that sometimes I used to just go straight home and cry. My grandmother was always there to comfort me, though. She'd tell me I had to try to understand how they felt and forgive them. Oh, it was hard, I can tell you, especially when it got so bad that there were only a few kids who would play with me.

Some of the full-bloods came from Barrington where they used to live in their own environment and follow traditional ways. Yet I was always delighted when I'd be taken out into the bush with them. They used to show me all the plants and wild fruit you could eat and those you couldn't. Even today that information is valuable to me.

Anyway I might have been a bit too fat and big to beat them at running, but, mind you, I was good at skipping! Oh, yes. When we were having picnics I would always win the skipping contests. Funnily, all the kids would be barracking for me then. I remember there was a girl from Kempsey at one of our picnics and they put me up to skip against her and I beat her hollow. Oh, they were all with me on that occasion. But why I wasn't liked all that much, I would never know. It certainly wasn't because they were jealous of me for learning a bit quicker, because they didn't put any value on education anyway. We were all poor to some degree or other, and education was a luxury that not even their own parents thought much of.

The first school I went to was the first school at Purfleet. A missionary, Miss Oldrey, had been sent up from Sydney and they'd built her a house. She applied to the government for a school and got the return offer of '£10, all requisites and a teacher — *if* the Mission would erect a suitable building'. Well, the money was raised and the people built that school. It was mainly built by my own grandfather in 1904 with a Mr Belford from Glenthorne. In those days it doubled as a church on Sundays. My grandfather split the shingles for this place as well as our own home. He was a real craftsman when it came to those sorts of things. He even adzed all the timber for the floor and walls. It was no mean feat.

The school was originally just one big room with two windows and a door. Later a great big window was installed on one side and then, later still, a little extension added. The first teacher we had was Mr Williams. He came from locally — from the school at Taree. He used to drive out every day in his horse and sulky.

The paddocks around the school were still really rough

with stumps and trees in Mr Williams' time. Now, a lot of children in those days used to come down from Gloucester to my grandfather's school, because it was the first Aboriginal school built in the whole area. They couldn't go to a local school. The law in New South Wales was that, if a 'European' parent objected, an Aboriginal couldn't go to that school. So we had to have our own schools and thanks to the Mission and our own hard work we got one at Purfleet. But, as a result, some of the children — the poor things — were actually just starting school at sixteen to eighteen years of age. Yes, they'd be sitting there in the first grades even at that age. Oh, it was funny then, but it is sad to think back on it nowadays. Anyway, on some days, Mr Williams would take the big boys outside and get them to dig up those stumps or cut down the trees. It must have been a blessed relief for them, even that. No doubt he did it on purpose precisely for that. It proved to be good in more ways than one, because the school finally got a really good playing area. So some good had come out of the poor things having to be there.

They got the stumps out by digging around them and then putting a lot of wood in the holes. Then they'd set it alight and burn the stumps out, you see. All night long there'd be boys hanging around the fires, having a high old time.

There were even some children who had to come from right out at Browns Hill, on the other side of Taree. Those kids had to make their own way to school and back each day past the local school that the law forbade them entry to! That's about three miles away. Occasionally one of them would stay with a local family and only go home weekends. I mention that because it's been said that Aborigines don't take to school much. That might be right in one way, but it was never made very easy for them either.

Mr Williams was a big fat fellow with great big jaws on him that seemed to hang down like a bloodhound. Oh, we used to make a great joke about this. But he was a good teacher. He was very strict, mind, and he wouldn't think twice about using the cane. I remember him especially because, for some reason, I just hated the thought of going to school while he was there. The next teacher was Mr Bruce, a short fellow and a whole lot different from Mr Williams, so I went to school gladly. I liked the look of him, so he had to be better, didn't he!

I was about six when I went to school and I loved it from the start. I used to even cry to go! Anyway, this Mr Bruce was really unusual because he allowed the tiny tots who were too young for school to go along. The only condition he put on it was that the older children had to take care of them. You know, I've always thought that a good idea. It helped the very young children to get to know what school was really all about . . . not something you had to be scared of.

There are still a few one-teacher schools in the country, but with so many leaving for the city, they will soon disappear. Oh, our school has long been closed and the children now go by bus to town. That has different problems.

Anyway, Mr Bruce used to have to go down to the missionaries' house for a morning cup of tea. We'd watch him go off down the yard through a peephole we had in the wall. And watch out for him coming back, of course. You can imagine what sort of hullabaloo went on while he was away, yet how angelic we all were by the time he returned!

This particular day, after he'd gone, a girl called Sis and one of my aunts decided they'd have a corroboree while he was away. My aunt could play the Jew's harp, you see, by using her tongue and holding it between her teeth. Well, we all just plain forgot about the time, even the lookout who was supposed to be watching out for Mr Bruce!

Naturally he returned and heard all the racket going on. What we didn't know was that he knew all about that peephole and was watching us go at it. The first thing we knew was him making a lot of noise outside. Everybody jumped back into their seats and began to look so busy and intent on their school work. Well, he walked over and sat down at his desk and just looked around very slowly. After a while he said, 'Mabel Russell, you can bring that Jew's Harp out here and give us another tune. And as for you, Sis, you can come out and do the corroboree for me.' So my aunt and poor little Sissy had to go out in front of the class and play and dance. They looked so funny, now that they were trying to be serious about it, that everybody started to laugh at them. Do you know what that Mr Bruce did? He didn't treat it as though those two little girls were being stupid, oh no. He just warned the rest of the class that if they didn't watch, he'd give them all six cuts for being rude!

There was a little bush house outside the school where the boys used to have showers. They had to carry the water up there in tins in those days; there weren't any rain water tanks. Anyway, pulling all those stumps out, as I told you, was hard work, so the big boys used to come back and have a shower. The girls were much luckier. We used to be taken down to the creek by the missionaries. We didn't have to be told twice to run in and have a swim, either! Sometimes, we'd have five or six swims a day. I remember how the boys used to sneak down and steal our clothes, tie them up in knots and hide them somewhere in the bush, missionaries or no missionaries. So we'd have to scamper around looking for our clothes hoping that no one saw us. Talk about laugh! You read about that sort of thing in books, but it actually used to happen to us. The missionaries weren't very pleased about it, I can tell you, but they could never find the culprits, so what could they do?

The third teacher was a Miss Caldwell. I remember she came from Hay and that her own brother was a missionary to the Aborigines. She used to live in town and ride her bike out to the school. Every day, there we'd be, waiting for her to come along on that bike and hoping that she would let us have a ride.

I was always doing things for Miss Caldwell. I adored her! I hung around her so much she had to like me. Oh, I would've turned over backwards for her. Anyway, this one day I was down there to meet her and I literally begged her to give me a ride on her bike. She actually gave in and let me. Well, I'd no sooner got on than I crashed and came a real cropper. I was in a terrible mess. In fact, I think I broke my wrist without knowing it, because for years and years after that the bone would stick out. Anyway, from then on I was always afraid to go on a bike. I just didn't seem to have the balance. Even if I had friends push the bike along, I would fall off as soon as they let go.

Miss Caldwell was a lovely woman, really. She was always trying to do something for us girls, especially trying to teach us music. Oh, she was strict enough. Like all those teachers then, she didn't spare the cane. But she wouldn't hesitate to stay behind after school to teach us whatever we felt we wanted to learn. Me, she tried to teach music. She really wanted me to get on. And even if I wasn't much good at music, I used to appreciate her *efforts* at trying to help me. It was important that someone was trying to do something for you. You'd think, 'Gee, somebody cares what I do.' It made school more meaningful — somewhere you went not because you had to go or anyone cared what you did anyway, but because there was someone there who was really interested in *you*, in what *you* could do once you got there . . someone who cared about you for what you were, not for what you looked like.

Anyway, to get us more interested in school, she told us she was going to give a prize for the kiddy who lost the fewest days during the year. Oh, I thought that this was for me, all right. I hadn't lost a day before, and I didn't intend to start then. And a prize thrown in, as well! Yet, for all my determination, I came unstuck.

It was one day that I got up a bit later than usual. I hurried out for my breakfast so that I could still be on time to meet Miss Caldwell riding out from town as I always

44

did. But this day I found that my breakfast wasn't ready. Well, breakfast wasn't going to stop me from meeting Miss Caldwell! So I dashed off over to the school, without waiting to get anything into my stomach. Of course, I got there in time to meet her and to push her bike for her, as usual. And, of course, I was there at school on time. But unfortunately it didn't end just there.

There were three or four of us in the school who could read. I was the best. Anyway, this same day, for some reason, only one boy and I were there who could read, and he couldn't do it very well at that. When it came to reading time, I had to stand up and do it all. I don't remember what the story was about only that it was a very long one. Half-way through I fainted. It might have been the tension of nearly being late on top of not having anything in my stomach . . . I don't really know.

I woke up outside, being fanned madly by the other children. Miss Caldwell had sent for my grandmother in the meantime, and she hurried over and fetched me home. I kept insisting that I was all right to go back to school, but she wouldn't have that at all. Oh, I could see Miss Caldwell's prize slipping away from my rightful grasp, you see!

Well, finally, I managed to convince Gran that I was feeling well enough to go back. But when I got back there, I found that Miss Caldwell refused to let me back in! I pleaded with her, but she said no, I was too sick and should go home and lie down. I even tried to tell her that it was only going without breakfast that morning, but she wouldn't have anything to do with that excuse, oh no. Now I really could feel the prize slipping out of my grasp. I protested to her as much as I could, but back home I had to go to bed. It was no good. I was sunk!

What made it even worse was that, after that day, my girlfriend Annie used to get on to me about how she was going to get first prize and I was only going to come second! Oh, that hurt me. I was furious about it. But at least I refused absolutely to admit it. Anyway, finally the end of the year came when the prize was to be given out. When

Annie's name was called I thought my heart would break. She was given a lovely bit of material for a dress. I was so jealous and seething inside! But then, I heard my name called. I did. I couldn't believe it. I found myself being presented with a bit of material for a dress, too. Oh, that was something and, what made it better, was that both her piece and mine, apart from the colour, were the same!

The story didn't end there, though. There was an English lady at the mission called Mrs Carson. I had become her favourite. I know it sounds awful, but I was always doing things for her too. Oh, I was a terribly busy little person, I was! Sometimes I'd be so helpful that I'd irritate them. Anyway, kind Mrs Carson said she would make my frock.

Some relatives of Annie made hers. It was a nice little pink dress with just a yoke and sleeves and gathering at the waist with a waistband. But Mrs Carson's had a sort of lace overfrock and a lot of embroidery work on it. It was blue and so beautifully made that anybody could see it was much better than Annie's. So, you see, I really ended up with the first prize after all!

I only went to school until I was twelve years old. I was in sixth grade by then and still hopeless at writing. To me, writing was the least important. I could read and I could spell; I could really do arithmetic and composition, so what did I need writing for?

Talking about writing at school ... I remember we had a letter box on the back of the school door and we used to have to 'post' our 'letters' in there as we wrote them. Every second Friday an inspector would come over from Taree and read them over.

Anyway, years later I came across some of the 'letters' some of the boys had written. They were nearly all about people being animals. In one I was a kangaroo and somebody came along with a gun and wanted to shoot me!

I didn't stay in school long after Miss Caldwell left. My grandfather had died in 1912 and Grandmother couldn't keep me, of course. Education was a luxury.

46

ABOVE: At the wedding of the author's Aunt Rachel to Percival Mosley in 1909.
She is the child in the long dress near the bride
BELOW: 'The first motor car I saw was owned by Dr Gormley'
Photo 'The Good Old Days', Jim Revitt

ABOVE: Three generations are represented in this photograph taken in Sydney in the 1920s: Ella's grandmother, Ella, and Ella's Aunt Maria

BELOW: Part of Purfleet in the 1930s: the manager's residence, the mission house, and the church

This lone mangrove on a beach stands out starkly against the sky

ABOVE: The site of the Gillawarra Gift Shop
BELOW: Some of the pupils in front of the school in 1936

6
THE PIG SCREAMED
AND SO DID I

Some of those six years at school were a joy, others were bad. But it wasn't too long after I had left school that I wished those years had never ended. I had begun to know how hard life could really be. At least, during my school days, I had a home and security, people I knew as my family. They had cushioned me against not being accepted either as a white or as an Aboriginal. But things soon changed drastically for the worse after Grandfather died.

It had rained solidly for six weeks. The river just kept on rising. Suddenly Grandfather fell down with the flu which had been going through the area. It quickly turned to pneumonia and pleurisy. Oh, so many people died during that epidemic! One of my uncles died just a few days after Grandfather and another aunt a few weeks after that.

It was the same all over. We couldn't get the doctor over because the flood waters raged for weeks on end, and there weren't any built-up roads then. Grandmother was away at the time Grandfather fell ill. We had to send for her. By the time she managed to hurry back home there were two corpses lying side by side in her home — her husband and her son. It was so terrible.

She was alone now and still had the family to look after,

to try to keep together. There were five of us — four of her own and myself. The eldest boy was sixteen and just old enough to start work in the bush cutting sleepers. The three small children, two aunts and myself, would stand on the logs and try to help him, but we were no use whatsoever. We even had to walk miles to town just to get food. Fortunately, there was a very sympathetic man who had a four-horse team and wagon and he used to often drive us back to the settlement. I remember what a treat it was when he shared his lunch with us.

Oh, that was a sad, sorry and hard time ... a time when Gran felt it necessary to have that long talk to me about who my real father was and so on. If that wasn't enough for me, I was still having trouble because of the colour of my skin. I'd go to parties and be told by somebody to get out and go into town where I belonged. For the first time, I think, I was beginning to realise how much it had cost my grandmother to make a choice to return to live with the black people. No matter how much she had done for them, she still had the skin colour that she couldn't escape from, just like me. Both worlds could reject her, too. On top of that I was finding out how cruel people can be about your parents not being married. So everything was happening for the worst and all at the same time.

My grandmother finally couldn't cope and it wasn't surprising. My eldest uncle had to move to Kempsey to keep his job cutting the sleepers. My youngest uncle went with him and my aunts were being married. That left me. What had to be done for me?

She sent for her brother who lived at Gloucester. I had to just stand there and listen while she told him that she was going to send me back with him to live; there was no other choice. He lived on the Barrington, in the mountains behind Gloucester, and what followed was one of the loneliest periods of my life.

You know, I returned to the Barrington around there recently — sixty-two years after I had been taken there

48

as a twelve-year-old who had suddenly lost the only home she had ever known. And I could still feel the loneliness; I could still remember lying there dreadfully homesick and listening to the cry of the curlews.

It had been all so different — the way they lived; the way they spoke. I had just wanted to go back home. My great uncle's name was Cook, but they called him Mulakut meaning 'lightning' because he had once climbed a tree that had been struck by lightning. Anyway, there was no argument; I had to go with him, first by train to Gloucester and then, believe it or not, by a horse-drawn milk van that was the only thing that went regularly up into the mountains.

They had three boys and a girl already living at home. I was put in with the daughter, Maggie, and her two children.

Maggie did try to look as neat and as clean as she could, at least. She used to try to talk to me as a mother would and tried to understand what I was going through. There were plenty of parties I could go to with her, because she used to help at them. But I didn't like to; I was still too young and, besides, there always seemed to be lots of men who were drunk and rude. It was all so different to Purfleet. They talked in their own language mostly; fortunately it was Birripi, the same as ours, so I could cope.

I wasn't there for long before I was sent out to Coneac Station with another of the daughters to help her while she had a baby. That proved to be even lonelier, if that's possible. There I was, still only twelve, yet I had to ride the horse to bring the cows up for milking; I had to feed the animals; and I had to do most of the hard work around the house. I was on the go from morning to night. I didn't mind having to deal with the animals, I remember. At least with animals I used to be able to make believe that they were my own pets. I didn't have anyone else to play with.

There was one pig I was especially fond of. You know how attached to people pigs get. It wouldn't let me out of its sight. I suppose we were company for each other.

Anyway, one day they came for it to be slaughtered. That was bad enough, but when the man said I had to help him do it, I thought I was killing the only friend I had left in the whole wide world. I had to hold its hind legs while he slit its throat. The pig screamed and so did I.

At that place I was always being told off for being useless. They treated me as though I was an adult. There was no way I could manage to do all those heavy things they gave me to do — washing, milking the cows, mowing down the barley to feed the animals, helping with the huge meals that had to be ready by the time the men came in from work. And what really added to my misery was that this daughter got so moody that she was constantly making life even more difficult. I got so that I just had to have someone to talk to. So one day I talked to Maggie about it. She was visiting her sister, and knew just how moody she could get.

Anyway, when she got back to the Barrington, she got her brother to come back up with an extra horse, riding skirt and saddle to fetch me back. And that was that with the sister and me — at least, for a while, anyway.

From there I got a job with a Scottish family in Gloucester — the McKinnons. They proved to be really pleasant to me, and even treated me as one of their own. I earned six shillings a week, living in. I taught myself to sew my own clothes and I used to get the good makings of a frock for half a crown from the old Indian hawker who came around there with his wagon. I had determined that if I couldn't have many clothes, I was at least going to have them nice.

When I finally left the McKinnons, I didn't want to leave. The wife had been kind to me. She had even taken me to some of their Scottish gatherings and taught me some Gaelic. But, yes, my moody aunt sent for me again, because she was having another baby and couldn't cope alone . . . her husband had come down to Gloucester especially to beg me to go back. So what could I do? I could hardly refuse; after all, it was one side of my own family. Besides, I thought, it might have been my own fault the first attempt at trying to get on together. So go I did.

I was just the same the second time. It certainly wasn't through any fault of mine. She just wasn't a happy person I'm afraid. She wouldn't pay me. She would find fault with everything I did. She didn't try to protect me when the stationhands got drunk and talked stupidly to me. She didn't even bother to make sure I was safe from being molested at night. Oh, it was all hopeless. She was either out drinking with the men or she'd be looking after her own two babies. I'd just have to go to bed, and most of the time the doors weren't even locked. At nights I was frightened all the time.

As soon as she had her new baby, I wrote to Maggie to send the horses up again! But what actually happened this time was that the sister of this woman, a Mrs Martin, worked a swap. She sent her girl, Jess, up to Coneac and I went down to work for her. That worked out very well, and for a time I was contented again. Not that I didn't still want to go back home, though. I had been away three years and was still just as homesick as the day I had been taken away. I had written to tell Grandmother that I wanted to return, but she got one of the missionaries to write back for her, saying that as things were I still had to stay where I was.

Mrs Martin's husband insisted she have her baby at Gloucester, so we moved back closer to there, which suited me fine. Eventually she had twins, but by that time I had taken fate into my own hands and returned home whether Grandmother felt the time was ripe or not. But first I had a little trip that was to be my first experience of going out into the big wide world on my own.

I suggested to Maggie that we ought to go down to the Wingham Show. We could get the train down in the morning and come back in the evening, and nobody would miss us. But how to get the money, even for the train fare? Well, by this time, I had started to write to my father, as I've said. So I wrote to him and asked if he could send some money to the Gloucester Post Office and not to Barrington, as my great uncle would come and take me back if he found out.

So, on the big day, Maggie and I hurried into town. One of my aunts had asked me to buy some flannelette while I was in there. It was about sixpence a yard in those days, and she gave me a half-crown. Anyway, good old Dad didn't let me down. Sure enough, the money was waiting for us at the Gloucester Post Office, and off to the Show we went. The flannelette could wait for on the way back. I was too excited to be worrying about commonplace things like that!

Oh, we had a fine old time! The people we met at that Show and had fun with! We just had to stay over for the next day, as well. So I asked my father for his permission. He didn't mind at all. The only thing he was worried about was where I was going to stay. I clearly remember him saying, 'The only thing I can do is to lend some of the saddle lining again for blankets.'

Well, that was perfectly good enough for us, thank you. We went to a friend's place and made up beds for ourselves with our lovely, yellow, woollen blankets. What was good enough to cover horses was good enough to cover us!

Hundreds of people had gathered for the Show and stayed over. It took so long to get to places in those days, you see. Once you got there, it was more than likely that you had to stay overnight and go back the next day. Anyway, early next morning, Maggie and I had a quick wash in the river and joined our friends for the second day. There wasn't a train out until that night, so we didn't need to feel guilty about enjoying ourselves the whole day. Somehow Gran heard that I was there and got word to me that she wanted to see me. But how could I? . . . we had no money left, not even for the flannelette that I was supposed to buy. I thought I was going to have to go to

my father again, but some of the boys chipped in for our
train fares at least. So after all that time I was on my way
back to my real home.

Home again at last. I remember creeping up to the old
house so that Gran would get a surprise. Do you know
what? She wasn't home! So I had to hang around and
wait for her. That was a real let-down after all those years.

Finally she returned and saw me. At first she hardly
even recognised me. I had shot up since we last saw each
other. I was fourteen already. Then she said the words
that I had so badly wanted to hear. 'I don't think you
have to go back. You're grown up now.'

Oh, we talked and talked. She wanted to know everything. There was so much to tell her and so much to hear.
Now, whenever Gran wanted to know anything in detail.
she would always get us to sleep with her. We talked in
bed right into the early hours of the morning that night. I
told her about the work I had been made to do, about
the men at the station and their drinking. I told her how
frightened I had been and how I had decided to leave
there after one of the men had tried to get into my bedroom
one night while my aunt did nothing.

That settled it. I wasn't to go back. Maggie went back
on her own. I didn't even go back with her to collect
my things. I never wanted to see that place again.

As I said, it was years before I did go back again. I
never did see my great uncle alive again. Of course, it
wasn't horrible all the time out at Barrington. There were
things that I still cherish remembering: the beauty of that
rugged countryside; watching a catfish build its 'nest' in
a great ring of sand; watching a platypus going in and out
of its hole; catching sight of the animals in the bush;
planting trees. But, above all, there was always the memory
of how lonely I had been. I can never forget that.

I soon renewed the friendships I used to have with the

young people my age. We had to organise our own entertainment then. We had frolics — or dances as you would call them now — which went on to the early hours of the morning. What with that sort of thing and Gran being so busy nursing and delivering babies and so forth, I didn't see much of her at all.

It didn't take me long to learn, either, that things at home had changed a lot. There was a man who came to visit us a lot. I began to realise that there was something between him and Gran. Soon I became so jealous and possessive that I couldn't stand the sight of him in our home. I couldn't help it; it was something I couldn't control. Perhaps I was trying to compare him with Grandfather, which was unfair, I know. Oh, I used to get myself so miserable about this man! I couldn't or wouldn't see that Grandmother wanted and needed a husband.

It's sad that we all seem to go against our elders and fail to give them ordinary feelings. It was only when I had my own family that I really began to fully realise my mistake. She had been a good mother. She had looked after her family, loved them, worried over them, worked her fingers to the bone for them, gave them their training and education. Now all she wanted was a life of her own. It wasn't much to ask after all those years, yet I wouldn't have it. Oh, no.

It made me leave home again. I felt so rejected, so I got a live-in job in town with people who owned a music shop. They had wanted me to sleep in an old place out the back, an old barn of a place. But after the station incidents, I had been too frightened to do that, so I used to come home each night. But, when I returned, there was often nobody there. I felt that my grandmother was being taken away from me. One night I couldn't stand the pressure any longer, so I left and moved over to my aunt's house nearby. She was close to having a baby and I used to help her around the place when I got back from work.

Housework was very hard in those days. There wasn't any electricity or gadgets like you have now; everything was done by hand. Just doing the washing was a hard day's work without anything else. You'd have to get the copper going as soon as you got there, make the fire, clean out the copper, fill it with water which usually had to be carried, and sort out the clothes. Then you'd have to put some in the copper to boil while you washed some by hand, rinse them, starch some, hang them out on the line. Then there was the scrubbing. They didn't have lino on the floors then, just rough boards with a few mats lying around. You had to scrub those floor boards by hand. We used to get them smooth by scouring them with rough stones first. Anyway, I had been doing such chores since I was about five or six, so I never had much difficulty in getting a job. I was a quick worker and always recommended by whoever I had just worked for. This helped me earn my own money and to always be able to look after myself. You know, when I think about it, the biggest part of my life has been spent in other people's homes!

My grandmother received a letter from one of my aunts who lived in Kempsey. She was having a baby and wanted my grandmother to go over and look after her. Grandmother told me straight away that I had to leave work and go with her to Kempsey. She never left her daughters on their own for too long, especially when they were pregnant. This was at the time, too, that my eldest uncle had got into trouble over a girl and had been arrested. The girl had had a baby daughter but her family was strongly against any marriage and were suing him for maintenance.

The aunt had her baby, which was her first, in the middle of the night. Why it never seems to be in the warmer weather and in the middle of the day, I'll never know. But Gran and I managed, even if, without electricity, it was hard to see what we were doing.

We had to wait there a long time before uncle's trial came up. Inevitably, Gran took the baby in the meantime. That was typical of her, but frankly I was longing to get out and have a bit more freedom. Anyway, when the trial came up, the mother of the baby girl didn't appear against uncle, so the child was given over to the custody of the father. This made things a lot lighter for me and I was able to go out and get another job — first with a farmer's wife, then with the wife of a butcher who had had quite a lot of children. I enjoyed being with the butcher's wife because she was very friendly and used to tell me all her little worries and troubles. By then I was getting towards being a woman myself, so I could understand what she was talking about.

Anyway, Gran remarried while she was in Kempsey. I knew he was a good man, kind to her and hard-working, but I just couldn't tolerate him. This upset her, but there was nothing to be done about it. After that, we didn't see each other very much. Oh, just occasionally I would go and see her, but not very much. When everything had got itself sorted out she and her husband returned home, but I decided I wouldn't return. It wouldn't have been any good, because I was ready to pick an argument with him any time I could, even about nothing at all. So I remained in Kempsey.

I started to go out a lot, went a bit wild, and made many friends. I worked hard, had many heartaches. I became interested in one of the boys who later gave me a terrible time and nearly broke my heart, but thank goodness that's a closed part of my life now, even though it still hurts to think about it.

But this situation didn't last for long, because once again I was sent for. This time it was the aunt who lived near Gran who called me. There had been yet another terrible flu epidemic towards the end of the war and Gran's husband had caught it, just as Grandfather had. So my uncle and I hurried back on the train. They gave us masks at the station to wear on the journey and sent anyone back who even had a cold.

He died before we got there, the poor man. So did many others. There were deaths everywhere. Some of their bodies are just below the surface here in the cemetery, you know. It was shocking. And, of course, my dear grandmother was nursing people as hard as she could, even though she was grief-stricken to lose a husband again this way.

The Salvation Army was very kind in this crisis and went around with great cans of hot soup which kept many alive, I can tell you. Quite a few of us didn't get the flu at all, but once you did get it, there was a good chance that you would die of it.

Well, after that, I stayed home for a while to keep Gran company, but finally I returned to Kempsey. I had more friends there, more work, and quite a number of relatives anyway. I still wasn't sixteen yet, but I was becoming independent and set in my ways already. In a sense I had reached adulthood. Even so, I fairly soon got a bit tired of the 'high life' there. Oh, there'd been plenty of fun, a few heartaches and a bit of jealousy and all that. But for some reason my nerves started to go on me. I went to see about them and the doctor advised me to have a holiday. You know, get away from it all for a while. And that is how I got to Karuah.

I had a cousin living in Karuah, so I wrote off, and was soon in the train on my way. You couldn't go all the way by train then. You had to get off at Stroud Road Railway Station and go down through Booral with the mailman. Well, I got a lift with him, but first he had to do a few deliveries, so he dropped me at a hotel to wait for him.

I knew nothing about hotels then. I didn't know whether they would throw me out because I was Aboriginal or not. To my surprise, nobody did try to throw me out at all. I can tell you that was a great relief! Anyway, finally he came back and off we went to Allworth, getting there late in the afternoon. My cousin was waiting for me there, but the trip wasn't over yet. From Allworth you had to row down to Karuah!

Karuah proved to be just the place to recuperate in. There was plenty of time to do nothing, and I was coming along real fine, until the day I got bitten by a dog. Yes, a dog. It was in the town's store. I was standing at the counter waiting to be served, when a black dog rushed past with another dog chasing it. When the second dog got level with me, it just turned around and bit my leg! I don't know whether it thought I was the other dog, or blamed me for it not being able to catch the other dog. Whatever the reason, it still bit me. I carry the scar of that to this day.

Then there were the trips around the bay. I remember one we went on was down to Gangham Beach. The weather was lovely when we left. There were two launch loads of us, including 'Queen' Charlotte. She was my grandfather's sister. Her husband 'King' Billy Ridgeway had been famous in his day. He used to wear a brass plate around his neck; it had been given to him when Parliament had made it fashionable to call the elders 'kings'. Anyway, the 'Queen' was a grand old lady, I can tell you.

As we passed by Soldiers Point she told us that story about the Aborigines being poisoned at a feast there. I mentioned that one to you earlier. It made us all very sad. She said the man who did it was called Cromarty. Actually there's another story about that man. I heard it from one of my aunts when I was back in Karuah recently. She told me that the old people had told her that Cromarty would get them to help him split logs. They would put in the wedges and then he would tell them to put their hands in where the wedges had split open the wood. When they did so, he would just knock out the wedges and crush their hands.

Well, we finally got to Gangham and the men fixed the camp while the women fetched wood. It was a beautiful, deserted spot. And the shells . . . I've never seen so many shells in one place. They were mostly little eye shells, but we collected them and made what they called 'fly catchers'. You hung them from the ceiling and the flies would be attracted to them. Oh, they served their purposes, all right. In point of fact, practically all the houses in Karuah used to use them.

It was just beginning to get dark when the first drop of rain started to fall. Then it really came down. It poured and poured. I can tell you, it didn't take us long to be back in those boats and on the way back to Soldiers Point!

Now, the 'Queen' had a dentist friend who had a

weekend cottage at the Point, so we made our wet way up there. We got a fire going and started to thaw out, listening to the rain still sheeting down outside. It didn't let up for days. It was just determined to ruin our holiday. But why I mainly mention this is because I remember how the Aborigines would stand outside with a tomahawk or something in their hands and they'd chop at the lightning and ask the rain to stop. Or they could make rain by doing this, too. Anyway, one of the girls decided she would stop the rain that way. She stood outside shouting and chopping at the lightning and rain, and all that. I'll never forget how wet and miserable she was getting out there, but that rain just kept tumbling down. It certainly didn't listen to her!

Our next trip was down to Mosquito Island. It was a place that was full of oysters, and there weren't any leases that you had to worry about in those days when you went oystering. One of the lads, my cousin's brother-in-law, rowed us down. Her own husband had warned us that the lake could get very treacherous. He told us that the wind could get up all of a sudden and before you knew where you were there'd be waves pushing and gushing around you. But we didn't take the slightest bit of notice of him. That might have been all right if we didn't have two kiddies with us.

We got down to the island all right. It was lovely and sunny and bright. There were oysters everywhere. I'm afraid we gorged ourselves a bit, even me ... and I wasn't even all that taken by their taste. Consequently we left it a bit late to start back. And, sure enough, the wind did suddenly whip up on us and the lake suddenly started to become a boiling mass all around us. Fortunately, I was able to row and could help the boy with one of the oars. We had to hug the shore to keep as far away as possible from the fierceness of those waves. It was one of the most frightening times I've ever had, especially with those two kiddies in there with us.

It must've been by some miracle that we finally made our way back to the wharf. I've never been so happy to see a place in my life! My cousin's husband was standing there, really upset. He had watched the wind start to get up and the waves get bigger and bigger, and all he could do was to stand on the wharf and hope he would catch sight of us. I don't know who was more pleased, him or us. That was one experience I never want to repeat.

I was enjoying myself so much in Karuah that I ran out of money again. I didn't even have the fare back, so once again I had to turn to Dad. Besides, I wanted to go back home to Gran again and I knew he could help me there, too. I knew, you see, he would gladly give me the money, and I knew I could save face with Gran if I told her that I had largely come back for his benefit, since it was true that he did like me to come back after I'd been away for any length of time. Really, I was happy to get home again.

The war had just ended. I can remember that very well. We could go to domestic jobs as 'servants' (that was the Board's own term) and I had written applying for a job in Katoomba. The lady there paid at that railway station for my fare from Kempsey West to Katoomba so that she could interview me. I was to catch the train leaving on the night that peace was declared and the ticket could be used on that day only.

Anyway, that day everyone was celebrating — including the railways — and the station was deserted. So I never got to that interview and missed out. However, I did hear from a lady in Sydney and got a job. That's how I remember the end of the war very well!

7

OPEN AND BEAUTIFUL WITH NOT MANY PEOPLE

At last I had saved enough money to go to Sydney. I had no idea how to go about finding a job there, so I wrote a letter to a friend of mine in Katoomba. Her boss knew somebody in Mosman who needed a housekeeper and they arranged to meet me at Central Station when I arrived. Her husband was a bank manager, and she had four boys and a girl. I ended up working for them for a couple of years.

I was terribly homesick and lonely for the first few weeks I was there. You know, that's what I've observed about most Aboriginal young folk. They get so homesick that nine out of ten of them don't stick it out and go back home. Little wonder about that; a big, strange city is even more difficult when you've got dark skin. I found that out when I tried placing them in jobs much later on, and I always had a great sympathy for them.

I was even more homesick because it was around Christmas time when I arrived. But when I thought about it, I realised I didn't really have a home now back in Purfleet, so I forced myself to make my own way. So, instead of running away like I really wanted to, I got stuck into cooking a Christmas dinner! The trouble was that it was a gas stove and I knew nothing whatsoever about

61

cooking with gas. I was really afraid of it. Then I saw an old wood stove in a corner. I cleaned it up, packed some wood in and got busy.

When the time came for them to sit down to dinner, everything was cooked to a tee; the turkey was stuffed and baked to a lovely brown; the plum pudding had been boiled in a cloth in the old-fashioned way. I'll never forget those children as they followed me into the dining room to see the brandy poured over the pudding and set alight.

I was so pleased when the boss came out into the kitchen afterwards to thank me! He even wanted to take some pudding back to the bank so that he could show it off to a woman there who was always talking about her Christmas puddings. He was a real gentleman in things like that. He appreciated the things I did for him, so if he had any of his bank friends over, I'd bake a cake for him. It was a great help getting used to Sydney with such a family, I can tell you.

I got on well with their kiddies, too. The three small ones were great pals of mine, especially the youngest, Bill. He used to really love the boat ride when I'd take him across the harbour to have his hair cut. You know, years later I saw his name up on a plate in Macquarie Street. He had become a very well-known doctor. It reminded me of those early days in Sydney — some lonely, some joyful, some sad.

But, if you stay long enough, you nearly always come across some deep trouble in a home. If it's not with the children, then it's usually between the parents. In this case, the mother became too fond of the horses and drink. For some reason she was also insanely jealous of her daughter. It really became unpleasant, especially since the children would still cover up for her so that their father didn't know what was going on during the day when he was at work. Anyway, after I'd opened my big mouth once or twice and really put my foot in it, I decided it was almost time for me to leave.

While I was still in Sydney I got an offer of a trip down the

South Coast in a car and I accepted. We set off to go to Wreck Bay, but the car broke down in Bulli Pass and we finally had to be towed down the hill in the middle of the night. This was all quite new to me. All I was used to was a horse and saddle, or a sulky; but at least they always got you there. It took us so long to get to even Nowra that I was almost broke by the time we arrived there. Otherwise I would have got the train back as I was thoroughly sick of these things called cars and sick of travelling along roads and sorry I had taken up the offer!

Anyway, at Wreck Bay the people we were staying with lived in little shanties, which didn't make things any better. Most of their men were fishermen. I was intrigued by the way they went about catching their fish. One of them would stand on a high part of the coast, scanning the ocean for signs of a school. If he saw one he would raise the alarm and they would all rush down to their boats. Then everyone had to be on the beach or in the water to help haul in the fish nets. The fish were then hurriedly boxed and sent on to Sydney to the markets.

The lady I had gone with just went off one day, leaving me to get home the best I could. I had to haul in a lot of fish to get my fare back to Sydney, oh indeed I did! Finally I got the lorry into Nowra and the train back to Sydney. You wouldn't believe what I found when I got back to Mosman ... The lady who had graciously taken me with her on holiday had come back and taken my job and clothes! No wonder she disappeared on me.

Well, I found another job in Mosman, in a ham-and-beef shop with a man and his wife and two children. He had only one leg and he was a real drunkard. And it didn't take me long to find that out, either. As soon as the wife and daughter had a day off, I suddenly found myself in charge of the whole shop because the boss had slipped down to the corner for a drop of wine. That became the pattern every time the women had a day off, too.

He'd get so tipsy that, with his one leg, he'd fall over

and wouldn't be able to pick himself up again! I'd have to go and hoist him up. Well, I managed to stick this out for a few months, which I still think was a long time, by getting the family to divide their days off, but one day there was a real blue and I told them I'd had it. The trouble was I had to stay until I got another job. I didn't have anywhere else I could go in Sydney and I couldn't afford to put myself up in a guest house or somewhere. Oh, that was a particularly awkward time.

Finally I found a job in a laundry over in North Sydney. At least it was a change from doing house-work all the time, but the hours were long, very long. You know, these types of jobs were the only ones we Aboriginal people could get. Myself, I had wanted to be a nurse, but black people weren't allowed to hold government jobs then, and try as I might I was never accepted as a nurse. It didn't matter at all that I'd already had a great deal of very wide experience nursing people at the side of my grandmother, or that I used to read every book or the subject that I could lay my hands on, oh no.

Anyway, I used to travel to work in North Sydney by ferry to the old Milsons Point wharf. There was no bridge then. It was just being started, so I was able to watch over the months as those two sides came slowly closer to one another. Actually I was also there for the opening, which was a thrill. What a crowd was there! There was such excitement in the air. I had one of my aunts down at the time, so we went along. We managed to get a place at the end of the bridge where everything was happening. Suddenly a man came bursting into the centre of everything. He was riding a horse and was waving a fixed bayonet around. Then all pandemonium broke loose. People were shouting and jostling each other everywhere. We didn't know what was happening; it was all so fast. Next thing we knew the police were dragging this man off. It was over almost as fast as it had begun. We found out later that he was a member of the so-called New Guard and that he had galloped in and cut the ribbon before the Premier could. We went home laughing about that all the way.

When I was working at Mosman, I saw them building the zoo. I used to walk down there on days off. A friend of mine would come with me to Balmoral Beach, too; it was also within walking distance so we went there often. That was when the Theosophists were building their big amphitheatre there, facing the Heads, ready for when this Indian fellow was supposed to come into Sydney Harbour walking on the water. Their leader was a man named Leadbeater and I often used to talk with him. He lived in a big white house on a high part around Neutral Bay way. A friend of mine, who was on the trams, told me that Leadbeater rode around on a white horse and had little boys all dressed up and he saw them open the gates for Mr Leadbeater. My friend said he had no time for him after that.

People were booking seats for the event by paying as much as £100 in advance to Leadbeater. I think the authorities were cutting down on Asian immigration and they wouldn't even allow the Indian fellow to come here then. When he didn't arrive, the money stopped, so they turned the amphitheatre into tearooms to pay off the debt.

A short while after this I had to have an operation. I came back home to Gran to recuperate. When I recovered I took her back to Sydney with me. It was her first visit. She was more than a bit afraid of going because she had heard so many bad things about the place, how Aborigines had every right to be afraid of Sydney people and all that. She soon got over it! Oh, she really enjoyed it; it gladdened my heart to see her. There were so many even little things that she had never seen. For example, I took her along to a picture show one afternoon. When we got inside, it was so dark that she thought she had gone blind. I had to half-lead and half-force her to her seat! Then there was the Zoo and trips up the Parramatta River. She was absolutely thrilled. They tell me she had a few tales to tell all her friends when she came back home!

I still wasn't well enough to work full time, but I did odd jobs just to have a place to stay. People were very kind to me, in fact. I had a very good friend out at La Perouse who had to suffer the same 'complaint' as me — a white father and an Aboriginal mother. Lena was her name, daughter of Harriot Bungay, she was doing the same sort of thing at La Perouse that I did later at Purfleet. I suppose you could say it was giving a lot of time over to trying to help the people in any way you could. Like they did to me, the people used to come to her at all hours.

Lena was working for Judge Stevens when I got friendly with her. Even after the Judge died she continued to live with his widow. Lena called her 'Madame'. They were very dear friends in actual fact. Kind old Lena helped me later on when I was working with the Mission out west and had to go back down to Sydney for further treatment. She let me use her flat for the whole three months I had to be there.

Oh, La Perouse then was a much different place than it is today. It was open and beautiful with not many people; plenty of swimming and laughing. I clearly remember a sideshow they had at the terminus there. It had horses and monkeys and other funny little things. Oh, we had many a laugh at the sideshows out there, I can tell you. Some of my acquaintances even used to go shooting at one of the old army rifle ranges where they held tournaments. I started to go along with them just for fun and then got pretty interested in it. I'd come home with bruised shoulders, but it was fun. I even won a trophy for long-distance shooting, if you can believe that.

By this time, though, the Depression was starting and things were beginning to get difficult in Sydney. One day I got word that I had to come back home anyway. Gran was getting really sick and there was no one to look after her. I must admit that this got under my skin a bit at the time. After all, Gran's daughter was living next door to her and there were others virtually just around the corner. You see, I was young and was just starting to really enjoy being in Sydney. But that didn't matter to the family; they still insisted it was my duty to come back at a trot. Of course, it was. Even I recognised that and normally wouldn't have hesitated. But it was the way they put it — reminding me of what I owed them and all they'd done for me. Reminding me of all the things they'd bought for me when I wasn't able to do things myself. You know the sorts of things I mean. 'It was up to me to repay the debt I owed them,' they said. As if I hadn't done my darnedest for all those years trying to do just that!

You know, I'm sure this is where older people make their gravest mistake. They're always getting on to children, telling them what's been done for them and what's owed in return. We should forget about things like duty and do things out of love, particularly when it's children in a situation something like mine — not having a real family.

I don't need to tell you how very sad the next two years were as I watched the one I loved slowly deteriorating. Gran had had both legs bad since she was a child. She'd fallen into a campfire when her tribe abandoned her and then, she told me, when Grandfather was building the house, she'd walked on a loose board; it had swung up and caught the front of her leg. Now the bone was poisoned. It was decaying. But she wouldn't have her leg off, oh no. She was in hospital for almost nine months and for most of that time she was in fearful pain. But she was always bright, always. She was such a grand old lady. She'd come home to die.

I spent more time talking to her in those years than I think I ever had in the past put together. I mean, really *talking*. We talked in the language. She had such an under-standing about the old people, the true tribal Aborigines. She went right back to her childhood days and often used to say how she wished she had known her own mother — the tribal woman who had died and then the tribe leaving her behind as an infant because she had a white father.

I remember there was a drought for about two years during this sad period of my life. I had to go down to the well to draw water, carry and chop the wood. If that wasn't enough, I had to walk the two miles to town and do the shopping. If ever my father was in town, too, I made sure I went to see him. I'd grown closer to him during the time

67

I'd been in Sydney; he used to spend some of his holidays with me down there.

It was about this time that I became interested in the man who was to become my husband. I had known him for a long while but never had much to do with him before. He helped to bring the fish in from Forster and, while he was down, he'd bring us some wood and lovely fresh fish.

But I wouldn't get married, I told him, until after my grandmother died.

8
THE SCAR ALWAYS REMAINS

In 1932 there was a change at Purfleet. The number of people living there had increased to such an extent that an officer of the Aborigines Protection Board was sent up. He presumably came to explain that the Board had decided to install a Manager on the reserve ... someone to live on the premises and help the people, and all that.

What happened was that, because of the Depression, more of the people had to ask for welfare and had to come on to the reserve. So the Board had to have more control. Its policy then became one of 'concentrating on reserves all people of Aboriginal blood with legal powers over them ... They were not to be at liberty to leave without permission'. All right, but if that officer from the Board had gone about it a little less heavy-handed, it might have turned out that way. But he didn't and it didn't.

He came in like a tornado. He upset every single person on the place — putting a family out of their home, arresting a young man, giving people their marching orders ...

The young folk made for the bush; the little tots were so confused and upset that they just hung about their mothers' skirts and howled. He frightened all of the old people. They ran hither and thither speaking to one another in their own language. I tell you, it was sheer bedlam!

One part of my own family was being ordered off while the other part was sick in bed. I had come back to look after Grandmother who was very ill. I was also going backwards and forwards to my aunt who had just had another baby. They never used to go to hospitals much in those days, you see. They had their own bush nurses, like Gran, but she was too ill, so I had to take over as best I could.

Anyway, this particular morning — on the day that this person from the Board arrived — I went over to my aunt's place to chop her some wood and make her a cup of tea. There were only two rooms in her tiny little shack and her children had a bed in the front room right near the door. She was in bed in the next room. Now, their father used to keep his axe under the bed in the front room. I wanted it for chopping the wood and, as I bent down to get it, this man from the Board just opened the door and barged in without so much as a by your leave. The door just missed hitting me on the head; that's how small those rooms were.

Of course I got up very cranky and said, 'What do you think you're doing?' He replied, 'Do you know who you're talking to?'

I couldn't have cared less who he was. Just barging in like that, no knocking, no asking permission. And nearly hitting me on the head, as well; that didn't improve my temper about it. And I told him that in no uncertain terms. They say a few home truths never hurt anybody, but they did him. He gave me twenty-four hours to get off the place! Yes, right out of Purfleet!

I was so upset I went straight over to my uncle's place. But when I got there, I found that this Board person had also ordered him out of his own home. No other arrangements, or anything. Just pack up and leave straight away. He wanted that house for the new Manager, he said, and my uncle and his wife and children would have to find somewhere else to live straight away.

We were the first people to come to live there. We had done much to build up the settlement, and now this white man from the Board right down in Sydney had come up and ordered us off! Well, I was really fuming by this time, as you can guess. But my uncle calmed me down. He said that there was still plenty of bark and wood around; we had started anew when Grandfather had come out here and we could start again now. So he decided to go and ask the Trotter family if he could build on their property.

Mr Trotter not only gave him permission, but said we could build on his property any time we liked — and use whatever timber we needed. You rarely come across kindness like that. However, it didn't help the situation in Purfleet very much. That Board man had really got everybody's back up, not just those of my own family.

In the meantime I had gone to the teacher and asked her what I could do about being ordered off the reserve. You know what her answer was? 'So have I, Ella, so I'm afraid I can't help you!'

She had been told to go because the Manager was going to do the teaching when he came. She'd only been there seventeen years! Actually, if the truth be known, I didn't care too much about that. In all those years most of the people she taught still couldn't read or write.

One of my other cousins was also in trouble with this person from the Board, just because he had the nerve to have a go at him about how the children were being taken away from their homes by force and sent to Homes of one sort or another. He had cornered the Board man, and told him how terrible the system was — how they were scared that any day their children would be taken from them and they might never see them again. He added, '. . . and if you ever lay hands on any of my kids, you'll know about it!' So this creature from the Board had him arrested for using threatening language!

Looking back on it it's still hard to believe that all this was accomplished in only one day. That Board man could get around all right! There was Gran as sick as she ever could be and her relatives were all being either ordered off or locked up. I didn't know what to do. How could I look after her, if I wasn't allowed back on the place? I could have gone back to Sydney to work but I just couldn't

71

leave her like that. She was dying. Oh, it was upsetting.

A little while later I went over to see the relief missionary who was there at that time and asked him what I should do. He suggested we approach the new Manager, who had just arrived, how we could go about getting permission to stay on Purfleet. We did so, and the Manager asked the Board man. The reply was that if I apologised, he might think it over and let me stay. My immediate answer to that was, 'So I have to eat humble pie or I go, is that it?' But there was nothing for it. What else could I do? I had to write a letter of apology to that Board man — his name was Smithers, I remember — and request permission to stay on the reserve. I got somebody to do it, because I couldn't bring myself to write it in person. That would have really stuck in my throat. Anyway, we got word back that I had graciously been given permission to stay in my own place. Oh, such a favour that was. I knew I had to be careful, though, while Gran was still alive and needed me. I just had to keep my mouth shut.

You know, one doesn't forget these things. The people can't and don't forget. They can forgive but the scar remains. Because of that man's stupidity, the people came to look upon the new Manager as a monster, instead of a helper. They simply wouldn't have anything to do with him when he arrived. Yet it easily could have been so different.

A few days after the Manager, the new missionaries arrived and what a different welcome they got. The Manager even remarked on it the night he was asked to welcome them. He said straight out that no one in Purfleet cared if he had a drink of water or not, but when it came to missionaries it was a totally different matter and he couldn't understand it. We could. We knew just how kind the missionaries had been.

Not long after I came to tell the Manager all about what had happened before his arrival. He didn't make the same mistake, oh no. Even when he did the rounds, he would ask us all first if it was all right to come and visit, and that was fine.

The Manager's wife arrived soon afterwards and straight away I was given the offer of a job to look after them. That was good. It helped me to support Gran and some of the family. The trouble was that there I was in a position to speak my mind about things, but I had to actively restrain myself. Well, the day finally came when my grandmother died and I was able to let myself go.

The first thing I told the Manager and his wife was that I was a human being the same as they were and I wanted respect as a person. I don't know whether they took any notice of that at all, but we certainly grew to respect each other after that, so I think they might have.

Actually that Manager proved to the people that he was their friend. I think he did a good job, all in all. After him there was a procession of Managers. They came and went. Some were sympathetic. Some were hard. Some were arrogant, some weren't. Some used their great — yes, great — authority without first finding out what the people needed or wanted the most. Anyway, they stopped appointing Managers in 1973. And, even in that, they did so without the slightest bit of warning that might have given the people time to adjust.

The same thing happened as far as the missionaries were concerned. The last ones were there in 1971. His wife took ill and they had to leave. The Mission had other remote areas it needed workers for, so it couldn't replace them. One day they were there; the next they weren't. What happened then was that the man who owned the hotel became the most 'sympathetic' person around to whom people could take their troubles. It's one of the great tragedies of today. I tell people in the churches that they have fallen down on their job by not stepping into the gap left by the Manager and the missionaries. They ask me how they can help now. I honestly don't know. All I can tell them is that they missed a golden opportunity then and it's going to be so much harder now to do something.

The first Manager was a soldier. He and his wife were both

73

English and had been in India before they got the Manager's post.

He was a good enough man, but he was a soldier right down to his boots. Funnily enough that actually helped. It was during the Depression then and there wasn't much work around at all. But instead of letting the people drop their bundles, the Manager organised them along army lines. He called the men together and asked them if they were willing to work. The only payment was going to be rations, that was all. That didn't matter; they said yes. And, you know, they did such a lot of work around the place while he was there. They really had the place looking good. They split posts. They did all the fencing. He sent to Sydney for canna plants and to Queensland for wattle plants and they soon had gardens blooming. A big archway was built over the entrance to the reserve. They renamed the reserve and set its new title up in great big daring letters on the arch. It read, 'Sunrise Station'. They even erected a flagpole!

Another Manager came along a few years later and had all this ripped down. We were at war then and he reckoned the new name was Japanese!

Talking about the rations the people had to work for ... in those days they were eight pounds of flour, four pounds of sugar, a quarter of tea, a pinch of salt if you were lucky, a piece of soap, about four pounds of meat, and you had to make your own bread and anything else. Whatever material was there we used to divide among the women, and then help them to sew clothes. I finished up doing most of the dresses. The Manager's wife could sew a bit as well, and one of my aunts. But other than the three of us there wasn't anybody else in the whole settlement who could sew well enough. But somehow we managed to fix everybody up with one dress at least. The material was a print of some sort, but it was quite good. Oh, and we had a choice of colours, too!

I had started work for the first Manager's wife, as I've

74

said, in the ration store and in the house. She was a member of the Country Women's Association; that's when I first came across the CWA, in fact. She used to entertain the CWA ladies quite a bit. They'd come out from town and admire all the lovely and expensive things she had brought out from India. The bedroom suite had come from England and was a beautiful thing, all inlaid. She had lovely mats and carpet squares from India, all hand-woven. Most of these things you didn't see in Australia then. Her house was comparatively grand, too. It had a big verandah, doors and windows that opened properly, fully-equipped bathroom and, after only a short time, even electricity connected and a phone installed!

She and her husband were finally moved to Kinchela Boys' Home in Kempsey. But it was only shortly after that that she fell and broke her ankle. She sent for me again. Now, at that time, Aborigines weren't allowed to work in that place. Personally, I think they were afraid that we'd see how they were really treating our kids and stand up for them. There were lots of jobs, you know, that Aborigines weren't allowed to do, just because they had black skins, government jobs. But I've already gone into what the system was like in those days.

Well, so she had fallen and broken her ankle and sent for me. She had refused to go into hospital; she just wanted me to come over and look after things until she got back on her feet again. So over I went. I was once again the centre of an uproar. I never learnt who reported it, but when I got there I was informed that I couldn't stay because Aborigines weren't allowed to stay there where the children were. Do you know what that Manager's wife did? She turned around and refused to let me go. More than that even. She threatened to leave herself if they made me go. I clearly remember the phone calls she had with Sydney, and they were ordering her to get rid of me. All her reply was, 'If she goes, we go. She's the only one who knows what to do. I wouldn't be happy with anyone else!'

Finally she actually won. They let me stay, rather than lose them. I was pleased to stay under the circumstances, too. Oh, it wasn't that I owed them anything. They'd already got a good deal of work out of me. No, I stayed because I knew I had to. I had to show that a colour bar like that had to be broken down. I had to show them, whoever they were, that colour is only skin deep. They didn't even seem to realise that obvious fact, even though this Manager's wife had begun to realise it and to accept me for what I was, not for what I looked like. The 'they' I'm talking about is the Protection Board, as it was, and all the people who revolved around it in all the different ways.

Anyway, I lived in the cottage at the Boys' Home with them and had to do her job, as well as all the housework. I proved I could do the job as well as anybody. I had to help organise breakfast for the children and get them off to school. Then I'd have to take her in the ambulance to have her dressing done at the hospital. After that there was all the house work and then helping her in the evenings until she was able to do some of the lighter things herself.

Finally I had to go home. I'd lasted a month and I felt I had made my point. But I had my own home to look after, too, and my own family.

Let me tell you about the second Manager then. He was raw Scottish with a broad accent. For some reason or other he was determined to get his knife into me. He was the one who made my dad move on and had others moved away from me. He even sank to holding up my child endowment. I suppose I used to say too much. Oh well, somebody had to. By this time, anyway, I was going through a period in my life when I was prepared to fight anybody for what I believed in. I didn't have my grandmother to consider and I was determined that I would never eat humble pie again. No doubt it was because I used to work for myself and wasn't a charity case that had to depend on the authorities for help. I saw things in a different light and, quite frankly, was game enough to stand up to them. Whatever the reason was, this Scottish Manager used to get terribly upset about me.

76

Still, even he had his amusing moments. For me at least. In school, for example, the poor kiddies just couldn't understand his accent, and then he would go on to think they were slow. He'd ask them to spell 'cart' and they'd all say 'c-a-r-t'. Then he'd bash them anywhere with that cane of his, shouting, 'That's nae how ye spell "cart"!' So all the poor little things could do was admit they couldn't spell 'cart'. He'd go to the board and write 'c-a-t'. Yes, 'cat'!

Or he'd say 'spuun' and want the kiddies to say it after him. They didn't have any idea of what he was talking about, so he'd bash them again and then go and write on the board 's-p-o-o-n'! I mean, it's funny to think back on now, but it really wasn't very funny at the time. He seemed to pick out one or two of the children who he'd punish all the time. One of my own and a couple of my aunt's got that sort of treatment. He wouldn't stop it, either. It wasn't just that the man was a fool, but that he was doing untold damage to the education of our kiddies.

Yet the authorities wouldn't hear a word against him. They didn't want to know, and besides they never bothered to listen to us. We were just helpless.

One day this second Manager brought a spiritualist woman up from Newcastle. Kate he called her, I remember. She was a funny old thing, really. Anyway, they used to have seances at night and invite Aboriginal women along. One night they invited two of my own friends along. One had just lost her mother and the other her sister. Old Kate told them, 'You come along and you'll hear them talking to you.'

Well, that's the worst thing you can suggest to an Aboriginal. They wouldn't come within cooee to hear a ghost talk. So they came and told me about it. Now, I understood the Aboriginal fears and I was in the Mission by this time, and was definitely right against anything like spiritualism that was outside the church. So we sat down and we wrote and complained about this situation to the Protection Board. We were also helped by a local farmer named Johnson, who was a J.P. and who was very sympathetic, as he had known the local Aborigines all his life.

Eventually someone from the Board arrived and organised a meeting to see if he could get things ironed out. Oh, he said that the first one he wanted to call at this meeting was me and the other two ladies who had sent the letter. That was a lot of rot too. When the meeting came, he let the Manager have his say first, and then he got up and said to us, 'Well, as a Christian to Christian, I want to say that we all should bury the hatchet right here and now and forget all this.' I thought, yes, bury it in your head! Oh, I was hopping mad. We all were. So we cornered that Board man after the meeting. He was a big person and he tried to push through us, but we wouldn't let him go. I said, 'Look, you've got to do something about this Manager; you've got to remove this spiritualist!'

You know what his reply was? 'I can't do anything more about it. Mrs M   is so ill. You wouldn't want me to upset her, would you?' And then went on his way. Upset *her*?!

ABOVE: Three of the houses on Purfleet about 1937
BELOW: The Mission Home and house at Purfleet about 1937

ABOVE: The old punt at Forster
BELOW: Mr Ridgeway outside his hut with chairs he made out of cabbage tree stems

Mary Ridgeway with her daughters Nita and Marcia, photographed in front of their house

The author and her father at the zoo when she was working in Sydney

9

'I'LL PRAY YOU OUT OF HERE'

Soon after the government started giving child endowment to everyone ours was taken from us. The Protection Board said that the Family Endowment Department, as it was then called, had to stop paying it to us and pay it to them and they would spend it for us. They would allow a few 'approved cases' to spend it under supervision.

The story I heard was that a woman in Sydney had her endowment stopped for ages and, when she finally got it, she was supposed to have gone all over Sydney in a taxi. Just because she was an Aboriginal they punished every Aboriginal woman. I don't know why they didn't just punish her or punish *every* woman, it would have made more sense. The Board said we were 'squandering' our endowment money and they were going to look after all money paid to us.

Well, that meant that my endowment went to the Board which sent this pink slip of paper to the Manager who would pass it on to me and supervise how it was spent. You could only take it to a big store to be cashed as they had to send it to the Board to get their money. There was one time I had to wait six months before I got it, because the second Manager, that Scotsman, had just simply decided he would cut me out of regular child endowment.

It was as simple as that. I had to fight for six months to get it back.

Anyway, this day we were having a meeting to discuss the various problems on the reserve and the things that we wanted changed. The Secretary of the Board had come up for it, which was unusual in itself. Now I knew him to be more sympathetic in listening to us women than just getting his information from the Manager and I was determined that I wasn't going to let this whole child endowment business be swept under the carpet again. I mean, for all of us, not just for me. So, despite the efforts of the Manager, I managed to get the Secretary aside and went to town on him.

I told him how some of us had been waiting up to six months for it to come through and how it was so slow in coming anyway. The kiddies were going short of clothes, so what was the point of having child endowment at all if it didn't come regularly. I asked him to do whatever he could about it. To my great relief he said he would get right on to it as soon as he got back to Sydney. And he did. He was true to his word.

About two or three weeks later — it was on a Sunday morning — the Manager sent for me. I could see he was determined to have the last word on the matter. I remember he sent for me just when I was on my way to teach Sunday School, knowing it was difficult for me to come right away. Well, I made it to his house and he informed me that he had big news for me. I asked him what. He said, 'You've got your endowment through!'

I replied, 'Well, that's good. I need it.'

Then he informed me that the snag was I couldn't get it straight away, but had to wait until the end of the month. 'Endowment,' he said, 'is never due until the end of the month.'

That was well over three weeks away still! Fortunately I had enough presence of mind not to get too flustered. It was an effort, I can tell you, but I managed only to nod and then asked him how much was it going to be, because surely it would be quite a bit after all this time. He told

80

me how much it would be, and then he had the nerve to go on to me about making sure that it was only spent on the children — as if I was drawing it for the very first time or, worse, as if I had been caught not spending it on the children! There was more to come as well. He went on to inform me that he would tell me how I should spend it — not all at once, only a little at a time.

I went home and thought about this. I decided the only way I could handle the situation was to get back at the man, but not in a way that he could come back at me again.

So next morning I went into town. I trotted in to Connell's because they knew me. I always shopped there. I badly needed a stove and had wanted one for a long, long time. None of the homes had a stove then; it was left to the CWA to kick up a fuss about it much later on. All we had were open fire-places, and we had to try to do our cooking in them. All right, then, if the money had to be spent on what the children needed ... well, they needed properly-cooked meals. So I priced the stoves, until I found a fuel one I could afford. Then I told them to have it delivered to my house in Purfleet. I still had some money left over in theory, so I also ordered quite a few things like kiddies' clothing and such. 'Send the lot out to me,' I told them, 'and send the bill to the Manager. He's the one who's got my last six months' endowment. He'll pay!'

Well, he hit the roof, of course, when he got that bill. But there wasn't a thing he could do about it, because I had bought only things which were correct. He just had to pay up. And, you know, that was one time that I managed to stay one step ahead of him! I also made very, very good use of that stove, I can tell you.

Pretty soon after that his wife got very ill. The only thing I could do to help her was to go and visit her often. He seemed to change then. Finally she became so ill that she had to be taken away to hospital, so he couldn't stay on. No Manager was allowed to stay on the reserve by himself; they had to have their wives along with them, you see. I always said to him, 'I'll pray you out of this place.' He never liked me saying that, and I don't wonder.

81

The day that he left some of the women and I went across and helped him to pack. Oh, he was so good and so kind, then. The next day the *Manning Times* had as one of its lead stories all about how Ella Simon had done so much for the Manager of Purfleet. It didn't half wrap my name up! If those people had only known about all the fights he and I had, and how I just felt I had to beat him!

His poor wife died some years later. Actually I met him in Taree well after she had passed away. Do you know the first thing he said to me? 'Do you remember the happy days we had at Purfleet, Ella?' I looked at him in amazement. I must admit that I was thinking, 'Yes, I remember the happy days when you had my own father thrown out of my house and off the reserve, and how you broke my heart when he died soon after. But it doesn't matter now, because my father and my husband are dead, your wife is dead, so I suppose we're just as lonely as one another when it all comes down to it.'

So that was how my house came to be the only one in Purfleet that had a proper stove, except for the Manager's place, of course. As I said, we managed to get stoves in the other houses after we'd joined the CWA. Even that came about in a funny sort of way. We'd formed a CWA branch at Purfleet, and, actually, I was the first President. At one of the very early meetings we had, some white women from Taree suggested we raise some money by cooking and then selling some cakes. We told them that wasn't much use because we had no ovens to bake cakes in! All we had were the open fires. They were absolutely amazed. The President of the Taree Branch, Mrs Hickson, said, 'You mean to say you haven't got stoves?!'

At a meeting shortly after that one she confronted the Manager about it. He wasn't the Scotsman, but the one who came after. He had been a missionary, and had taken over managing the place. Even so, he got a bit upset about being asked by the CWA of all people why we didn't have stoves. It didn't matter if he did get a bit upset. Within a few months we all had stoves! It just goes to show that you only have to be the right person asking.

Do you know why they hadn't put stoves in the houses up until then? I honestly believe that they hadn't bothered enough so that they thought we had no need or use for them. One of the Managers we had even used to come over to my place especially to watch me cook in a camp oven. He thought it was quaint because he had come from America and had watched the Red Indians cook in the open, but had never seen a 'native' using a camp oven! Oh, I could cook in a camp oven all right. You had to make your bread and you had to make your stews. What else could you do? It was a case of having to make do with what you'd got. That's why I could cook in a camp oven!

The houses didn't have bathrooms either. They *never* had bathrooms. Even when the new houses were built, there was just a shower put in. You had to be an acrobat to use it. I think they were old army affairs. Really. If you wanted a shower, you had to go and fill this contraption up with hot water and then you had to pump it on to yourself while you tried to lather up with the soap at the same time. Quite honestly, it was almost impossible for yourself, let alone trying to manage children under it. The poor women . . . it was much easier just to pour some hot water into a laundry tub and bathe the kids in those. I saw many a baby bathed in the wash-house in a tub that had just been used for washing the clothes. So the word got around again that the people are somehow dirty because they wouldn't use the showers that were put in the new houses. Honestly, anything was better than trying to cope with those pumps.

Even those showers went the way they should have soon after we joined the CWA. Everything seemed to happen in just one year — 1960. It was as though the heavens had opened. We got our stoves. We got a footpath. Suddenly there was water and electricity and even the pre-school was started. The Gillawarra Gift Shop was opened on the reserve and a Parents and Citizens' Association formed, as well as the CWA. At last we could talk to people who were keen to really listen to our state. They were country women. They knew what we were talking about. Many of them had been through much the same thing at one time or another. I used to call it the sympathy of bitter experience.

The funny thing was when they put the footpath in. We were determined to get the footpath because the kiddies had to walk along the street. I even joined the Road Safety Council to try to force that footpath through for us.

One of the policemen from Tinonee used to take me to the Council's meetings and he was right behind me for this footpath. He was on the motor bikes and knew very well what danger those children had to go through to walk along that busy road.

Well, finally we got a footpath that went from the shop verandah up to the top house of the reserve, but there it stopped dead. Well, that was a start anyway. But they had no sooner laid that down, than they decided to put the water on. So up the footpath came while they put the water through — even pulling down my fence and trampling all over my precious garden. So they had to fix those up, too. They relaid the footpath. And that was that for a little while until they decided to put the electricity through to the reserve. So up came the footpath again!

They weren't setting the greatest example to the people, were they?

Our Gillawarra Gift Shop had a committee, and I was on it and so were some of the local businessmen. We started to make noises about having the footpath extended right down to the bridge, to the town. The shops had spread as far as us, too. But no, they wouldn't have that; there was no money available. I said, 'Are you going to wait until somebody gets killed, is that it?' You know, not long after that, a poor little girl *was* killed up on the top of the hill.

Then two men were run down and died after her, and another one half-killed. Then they decided to put lights here. I don't know whether that was supposed to be a compromise or what. Who knows? But that footpath . . . it still ends in the same place to this day.

Yes, the CWA really started to get things going for us. We got the pre-school for the simple reason that the CWA believes that every branch should have a pre-school. We applied to the Save the Children Fund to finance it. It was as simple as that to get one! Thank God for the CWA. Then there was the gift shop. We got it this way . . . as I said, I was the first President of our Branch then. Oh, I was learning quickly, I can tell you. I was starting to get more hide. So I went to the Manager and I passed on to him the decision that our members would like the empty Ration Store for our CWA meeting room and also to start a gift shop. The Ration Store was not used after they eventually allowed ordinary pensions (1959!), so we wanted to make use of that empty building. It was just standing there, not being used for a thing. Well, was that possible, I wanted to know from him. He said, 'I think it might be, but you will have to do it up yourselves. We haven't got the money to pay for it.' That was fair enough for us. We hopped into the challenge. That store became our newest project.

I think just about every CWA branch on the north coast of New South Wales sent us cheques to set ourselves up and get the shop going. I got one of the boys who was working in town to cement the floor for £10. We got two extra toilets that weren't being used in empty houses on the reserve, too; all we had to do was to pay for their removal to the shop. Then Apex appealed to their people to come out and paint the place. It was at this stage that the Board chipped in. The Manager graciously informed us that the Board would supply the paint — since we were

85

going to supply the labour. Oh, and that was just about typical of the Board. You never got things for nothing.

Well, anyway, the Apex people came and not only did the painting but also filled in the floor. We even managed to borrow money from the bank to open our own gift shop, and the local Peters icecream factory gave us cinders to fill in an old well that was around the side. So, as I said, suddenly we seemed to be moving, standing up and getting things done for ourselves with the help of people willing to give us a go. That was definitely the influence of the CWA.

Finally the great day of the grand opening arrived. We had a huge barbeque. The Apex people even came out and cooked the steaks which they sold for us. What did it matter that it was pouring rain? Here we were opening the Gillawarra Gift Shop, the CWA room and the pre-school all in one day! Oh, and weren't there a few people there, too. I can tell you that there's only been a few times in my life that I've felt more proud. It was 27 April 1960.

At first we had two women running the shop. They were supposed to be the manageress and her offsider. They only lasted a few months. They lacked the necessary experience and ordered far too much of the wrong things. We couldn't sell them. After only a few months the shop was already badly in debt. So I stuck my neck out and went to try and work it properly. It meant I had to work practically for nothing at first — just the bare expenses of living. But I didn't mind that too much and gradually I managed to get it out of debt and running smoothly.

I hadn't known the first thing about shops and I can tell you I was more than a little afraid. I'd given up my job to help things, and there weren't too many of them around, either. Fortunately the Shop Committee did everything it could to help me, including time to get it all worked out. You know, I think we only ever had three other Aboriginal people interested enough to get on the Committee. I think they were frightened to commit themselves in case they made a dreadful mistake. They were a bit afraid of handling money. Who can really blame them? None of them had ever had much opportunity of getting used to handling it! I was just as bad, but someone had to learn. Something had to be done.

Of course, the Manager was on the first committee and he handled the money. Mrs Harper took over when he was dismissed. Then there were myself and Stella Russell at first with two other Aborigines — and four very kind businessmen from Apex. We had a proper constitution and there had to be equal numbers from Purfleet and outsiders. One of the men was a top accountant and another was a chemist. At the start they helped me keep the books and purchase the goods. If I made a mistake, which was pretty often in those days, I could always ring up one of them and get some advice. But slowly I became more and more confident and able to carry on on my own. Soon the shop was a going concern. Not a wild success in money terms, but at least *going*.

That shop was started without government money. We had a bank loan to pay off and it was run like a proper business gradually being built up until it was beginning to show a profit as more people got to know about it and came to buy.

I remember the time I had to go to Sydney for my operation. I'd got tired, you see. My husband had died and I had been working so hard. Anyway, I was away for six weeks, so we had a woman come in to take over while I was away. The day I walked back into that shop, she almost cried out, 'Thank God you're back. I've had it!' She never came back again. Finally we got a couple in for a whole fifty cents an hour to help out. That's how poor we were to start. We had assets but never ever hard cash.

The branch of the CWA closed down. That was such a pity, after all the good it'd seen done on the reserve. The women just lost interest in it after a while. But that at least meant we had two rooms for the shop then. We got counters, some good showcases and put such luxuries as lino on the floor. You know, it started to really look like a proper shop after all! Then it started to become a meeting place for the women. They'd come and sit around sipping their morning or afternoon cups of tea and discuss their problems. It was starting to be more than just a shop. If that wasn't all, I had become a JP by then. That meant the people brought forms in to be filled in, and also whatever special problem they might have. The shop was starting to be a miniature welfare place in its own right. It was also a calling place because it had the only phone there — to call the police, or the doctor, or the hospital, or the social welfare service in Newcastle. Everything began to revolve around the Gillawarra Gift Shop! I started to find that my name was being mentioned for everything — even taking and giving messages about jobs. You know, seeing they got to the right place at the right time on the right day and that they got the right money. By then, of course, they had taken the Manager away. If it hadn't been for that little shop, God knows what would have happened. We would have been isolated from the world.

Yes, the Board had moved the Manager out because they had reckoned that equality had come in, you see. That the Purfleet people had to find their own feet and do things in their own way, just like everyone else. Just like that without any warning. It sounds very easy, doesn't it?

I finally got out of the shop after ten whole years. I suppose it was about time I retired, anyway. I was getting old and sick of it and I became pretty fed up with everything that was going on in latter years. It wasn't only that some people had started making a convenience of me and the shop. What really worried me most was the Black Power movement. They came into Purfleet. One day some of them came up to me and actually asked what happened to the money from the shop.

Well, it wasn't my business to tell outsiders what we were doing in the shop and how we were doing it. If they wanted to know that they were perfectly welcome to go to the meetings. And this is precisely what I told them.

I remember we had just applied to Canberra for a loan for a bigger display window — quotes, blueprints, and everything. Anyway, a short time after that, two of these Black Power people and their friends came up to me again and informed me that 'the people' wanted the shop. They didn't want white people on the committee any more. Well, that finished me. I told them I was leaving too.

It was against my principles not to have a mixture of black and white. They wanted it run by Aborigines only. I just didn't want to work under an all-Aboriginal committee, and that's the truth. I felt this was just another colour bar. And I had the feeling that these Black Power people just wanted to get the people all to themselves. They weren't trying to assimilate them. Doing this wasn't assimilating them. It was just getting them back where they were, and I just couldn't be any part of that.

10

THE LAST OF THE FULL-BLOODS

Thinking of my old home makes me think of old Sister Morcombe. We used to call her in the language, Knurian, which meant sister. She was the one who looked after us girls when we were tiny tots. It was expected that she did in those old days. The old Aboriginal people always played their parts in the community. They had to take the children and teach them the correct ways.

One day each year we would be woken up before the crack of dawn and taken to a sort of 'look-out' out on the Forster Road where we could see the ocean. There we'd sit by a fire and have to wait for the 'dancing sun' to come up. I mean, it really was dancing on that day. It shimmered on the waves and looked for all the world as if it was dancing over there. It was only to be seen on Easter morning. How they knew it was going to happen I don't know. Like all their deepest secrets it was only for a few of them to know. And, like so many of their secrets, it has died with them.

Then there was the Barlow family. They were all full-bloods. Paddy, the brother, was called Cookal by the tribe. Emily, his sister, was called Burrang. Then there was Lizzy whose tribal name was Walka. I remember Cookal was a shy sort of fellow and very quiet. Yet he was a big man with a very husky voice — what I call a typically shy Aboriginal. He was 'Keeparra' (law man), so he had to be quiet where women were concerned. He used to do a lot for the priest's garden, but he always seemed to be a loner somehow. Walka married a Queensland full-blood man. They had a child, and do you know what they called him? 'Boy'. Yes, just 'Boy'. He grew up so shy that he used to get up the back of his father's coat when his father stopped to talk to anyone, and stay there hiding his face. He couldn't even bring himself to look at anybody.

Burrang was very short and very fat. She played the concertina really well. She'd play it at dances. Oh, she used to drink a bit and was a real wag. I remember she was always talking about some gold she could find around the Black Flat Mountains. She used to tell the young men that, if one of them would marry her, she'd show him where they could find it. But she never did catch a husband, not even with that bait!

There was also Jack Button who married Rose, a full-blood from the Worimi Tribe. Jack was one of the funniest men I've ever known. He could entertain you for hours with his funny tricks. He liked to paint his body with clay and to roll up pieces of paper with kerosene on them and set them alight on his body. You'd swear he was burning up. Oh, it used to give us kiddies a lot of laughs, until one of the boys got his feet badly burnt when he kicked this ball of fire. Jack with all that clay over his body and hair looked a really hideous sight, but he was funny. One night the police gave him the authority to clear out all the Aborigines' houses. They were pulling his leg really and I suppose it was amusing at the time, but the old full-bloods didn't think it was funny at all when they found out. They had their own laws which had to be adhered to and this was the height of disrespect, so they took the Bundi — the big stick with a large head on it, like a club — to him. Poor Jack, he really copped it.

He was from the Barrington Tribe. He even built an aeroplane once. He'd seen a picture of a plane at the show and he'd copied it from memory. Would you believe he made it out of an old bike frame! It had some sort of material sewn to the handlebars and was the funniest thing you ever saw. Well, he took it somewhere over near Browns Hill, wheeled it up to the top and then came flying down! He ended up almost wrecking himself, as well as the bike! He must have had nine lives.

Another thing he used to do was come downhill riding on the front of a cart they used to borrow from somebody. He'd have his feet up in the air and be tearing down like mad. There'd be poor Rose, his wife, sitting in the back and hanging on for grim death. How he never killed them both, I'll never know. It was just his ways of amusing the kids. Oh, we loved old Jack.

Then there was old Tommy Boomer who lived in a camp at Saltwater. He'd mostly go and live there during the cold months. The tailor would be on then. He made his own fishing hooks and everything. I remember I visited him there and he had his own invention of a fishing line. He had this stick which he had smoothed off. He had a rag around one end of it and a hook at the other end, fitting snugly into a little crevice in the stick. Then he wound the line around and around the stick and brought the end back through under the binding. He was such a powerful old man that he could cast this thing right out over the waves. I saw him do it. All of a sudden I saw this great big fish taking the hook. It was attracted by the rag. The tailor in those days were simply huge; he'd think nothing of pulling in a four or five pounder.

Then he made a good fire and we all had a great feast. He shared everything he caught. He was such a dear old fellow. You know, he was killed later walking along the railway line. He used to have the habit of walking down the train line to Wingham, because it was easier that way. The trouble was that he was quite deaf. This day he didn't hear the train coming and it just ran him down. Anyway, I remember him with a great fondness and always will. He was part and parcel of days in my life that were always so enjoyable. Collecting all those pipis and black periwinkles while he was out catching those fish, and then boiling them and cooking them all up. We enjoyed those days.

Albert Lobban and Arthur Marr. Arthur was better known as 'Bossy'. Both of them were really good cricketers. Albert was a fine figure of a man — a big, strong Aboriginal. Dr Stokes at one time invited Albert to meet his brother who had a practice in London, but had come out here for a visit. Dr Stokes was keen for this man to see what a fine specimen of a man an Aboriginal could be. Poor Albert had to undress in front of them while Dr Stokes pointed out this and that about the typical build of a full-blood. When they got to his feet, Dr Stokes informed his brother not to take any notice of Albert's toes. They weren't typical. Oh no, they were like a white man's toes, because they were crushed together from wearing shoes! No, these were definitely white man's toes.

Dear old Albert, he used to laugh like mad when he told this story to anyone about being studied by two doctors and their discovering he had an Aboriginal body but white man's toes!

Now, Bossy, he never wore boots or shoes. He was the other way about of the two — his feet were broad, really broad. No corns, no bunions, or anything. He lived to be a very, very old man, in fact. He used to give a lot of fatherly advice to people at Purfleet. He was helpful to me when I was trying to cope with all the nursing that had to be done around the reserve, I can tell you, whether it was a birth of a child or a death. Funny thing, though, he would never ever touch a dead body. I remember being called one Sunday morning to attend to a full-blooded man who had died during the night. Bossy was the only one I could see to come along with me to help. He did, but he refused to touch the body, no matter what. He told me later that it was against his tribal laws for him to touch a dead body.

Then there was the time that his own daughter was

93

having her baby. The woman who was to nurse her panicked and ran away, so I had to hurry over to minister to her. Bossy came with me. But when we got there he suddenly informed me that it was against his tribal laws to touch any of his relatives having children either! It was a great help to be told that then! Anyway he told me what to do, so with the help of him talking, I managed to get the young woman through it all right.

These were typical of the full-bloods I came in contact with. There were many, many others, of course. There was Jim Moy, for example. He was a real man of Purfleet. It was he who kept the tribal law and order around the place. He was not only very tall, but strong and thickly built with it, so he was just the man to keep the tribal system alive. I guess he would have been about sixteen stone. He was married to another full-blood, and they had three children. His wife died young and the children were left with old Granny Moy.

There was no fooling around with old Jim and everybody knew it. He carried out the law to a tee. If anyone of those people did something wrong, he would severely punish them. There was no worry about that. He demanded total respect for the Aboriginal law and teachings. Even when strangers came to Purfleet, Jim Knuppy — or Knuppy Moy, as they used to call him — had to meet them and pass them as being all right first.

When the Protection Board appointed a Manager and made Purfleet their first 'official' station, it proved to be the finish of poor old Jim. Almost straight away he began to deteriorate. He'd lost his position of authority, you see, and had nothing to live for anymore. Anyway it wasn't too long after the Manager arrived that he got so sick he had to go to bed and stay there.

Now, this is a thing that a full-blood dreads, having to lie helpless in a bed. To them it means the end of their endurance and usefulness, the end of their independence. The Manager got a doctor over to look at him. I know for

94

ABOVE: An Aboriginal marching girls' team, the Purfleet Aussies, taking part in a parade through the streets of Taree

BELOW: The author's husband and sons returning home for dinner on a farm

Ella Simon, photographed at the Purfleet Mission House in 1947

ABOVE: *Back row:* Len Mitchell, Arthur Marr—known as 'Bossy' Marr, the man who did all the helping with mothers and babies—and Arthur Ridgeway. *Front row:* Charlie Bruce, missionary Ron Marr, and Glennie Crinton
BELOW: Pastor and Mrs Frank Roberts *(left)*, Frank Roberts, Jun. *(right)*—from Lismore; Mrs Ella Simon—from Purfleet; and two South Australian girls from Ooldea mission

A photograph of the coast near Forster

a fact that that doctor was absolutely amazed at such a build and physique. He was new and hadn't seen an Aboriginal before. Anyway, old Jim refused to go to hospital or even live in a house. He had to have his own bark camp and his own fire. So they built him a camp. Hospital was out, because tribal law said that no woman could handle a man's naked body. He said, 'I will die if I go away from my fire.'

Finally I was asked to look after him. It became a full night's work. One woman would come till ten o'clock and I would be with him for the rest of the night. His fire was his medicine. Oh, he did love that fire so much. He'd be sitting there by it, telling me tales of long ago when he was a good fighter. He was always complaining about his head and I commented one night that he must have been knocked out one time. He didn't get so much indignant at this as proud. He told me that no man had ever knocked him to his knees, except his own brother! A fight between the full-bloods would be a fight of endurance, you see. One would put his head down first and the other fellow would hit him as hard as he could on the head with a club. If he didn't knock the first man down, he would then have to bow his own head while the first man would hit him, and so on. Just as well the Aborigines have very thick skulls!

By this time old Jim was starting to go downhill fast. He asked me to go and get the 'Boss', as he used to call the Manager. When the 'Boss' came, Jim asked him to sit by the fire with him and told him that he had come to the crossroads of his life; he felt he could not go any further with his people. He went on to the Manager, 'Now they will have to go with you.' He had had a dream, he said, in which there was himself and the Manager standing at the crossroads and, in it, he had said to the Manager, 'Which way are you going?' He got the reply, 'I'm going south.' He shook his head and said, 'I'm going north, so the people must go south with you.'

He had an old blue blanket which he used during this time. Each night he would sit by his fire and he would tear a piece off it and put it in the fire. There was only

95

one tiny piece left on the Sunday morning that he died. They buried him in the cemetery out on Forster Road.

They gave him a proper Aboriginal burial. The Methodist minister took the first part of the service, but after that the women and children had to leave so that the initiated men could bury him properly according to tribal custom. They threw all the implements he had used into the grave with him — his precious bundi, axe, spear, boomerang, fishing line. His grave faced north for this was the way he was travelling. Dear old Knuppy Jim. He was really one of the very last. In a way he was the last. There were no more bundis used after he had gone. The last law man to use the stick with the big knob had gone.

Then there was old Jack Crinton, whose wife, Emma, had a girl by a white man. He used to carry out the initiations of the young men. He lived on the Dingo Creek, just outside of Wingham. I don't know how he knew when to come around for the lads, but he did. I remember he would come and wake them up in the early hours of the morning and then rush off.

And the old woman Topsy, who used to go off for a day and come back with some alluvial gold when she wanted to buy her tobacco and drink. Her drinking often got her into trouble but she never did show anyone where she found that gold. It was somewhere up the Johns River way.

There was also another Mary; she was a half-caste woman who married a full-blood, Angus Moran. They had two children — a boy and a girl. Mary had a sister, Helen, who married a Ritchie from Kempsey and a relative of the famous Ritchie (Sands) boxing family. I remember Mary had a brother who was called 'cricketing Charlie'. He was a very good cricketer and also a good climber. He left his mark on a few trees that grew around the place. A lot of Purfleet men were good cricketers, too. They loved the game. Apart from Albert Lobban and Arthur Marr and 'cricketing Charlie', there was Ted Lobban and Arthur Morcombe. Arthur came from the Wauchope Tribe. I actually saw him hit the ball right out of the ground at Nabiac. It sailed right over a tree and we all heard the breaking of glass as it landed somewhere out on the road. You can guess what had happened. My brother-in-law, Barney Simon, was a good cricketer, as well.

Then there was a man I used to know only as Harry. He became the best roughrider throughout all the showgrounds of the North. He later died in Sydney Hospital after he'd been thrown while rough-riding at the Nabiac Showground. Apparently his heart had moved out of its normal place and was enlarged. The doctor said it was as big as a bullock's heart. When he died they got permission to use his heart for research work.

But, of course, the most famous of all the Aboriginal sportsmen from around our way was Dave Sands.

Mr Sands had taken the Ritchie boys under his wing after seeing them fight. They took his name and became known as the Ritchie Sands brothers. Clem was the eldest. He had a bad mishap in one of his fights. His opponent died. This shook him up so much that he gave up boxing after that.

Percy was known as the 'Brown Bomber' or 'Bimble' to his Aboriginal friends, because he was so fast in the ring. He finished up going a bit violent and getting into all sorts of trouble with the police. They said he went 'punch drunk'. Actually he died only a short while ago and is buried in the Kempsey cemetery.

Of course, Dave was the greatest. He went to Britain and America and became recognised as world champion potential. They tell me he was one of the greatest boxers of all time. He was at the height of his career, and preparing for a title fight, when he was killed back here at home. Oh, that was a terrible tragedy. He was killed by his own lorry out there on the Dungog Road. He had invested some of his prizemoney in a sleeper-cutting business for the family. His father had been a wonderful sleeper cutter. Anyway, Dave was driving some friends and relatives out there when he went to take the wrong turning, skidded and rolled down an embankment. He was the only one out of all of them in that lorry who had so much as a scratch and yet he was killed. That shocked the whole of Australia, you know.

I went to Newcastle to his funeral. It was one of the biggest funerals ever held for a boxer, and' he was an *Aboriginal* boxer at that. His mother, Mabel, was one of the Russell family who had moved with my grandfather from the camp on the edge of the town to Purfleet in the early days.

As I stood at Dave's funeral among this great crowd of people, my mind went back to when he was small. One of the white boys who went to school with him used to take him along to the shop after school. The white boy could go in and buy a drink, but Dave had to wait outside the shop. He wasn't allowed to go in there. He had to stand outside while the white boy bought the drink and brought it out. He'd have to drink it out there, and then give the bottle back to the white boy who had to trot it back into the shop. That wasn't because Dave was bad, but purely because he was Aboriginal. Anyway, he was man enough, even then. He stood outside that shop and he drank his drink, and, what's more, he'd enjoy it.

I wonder what that shopkeeper thought the day Dave was driven up the streets of Kempsey in triumph and everybody, white and black, stood and cheered him? Or was it all forgotten just like so many hurts that have left so many scars on the people?

I've said before and I'll say again that that Protection Board gave the people more heartaches than protection. At one stage a man named Donaldson had the responsibility for our area. He was their Inspector and he wasn't really ever accepted by the people. In fact, it got so bad that his name only had to be mentioned to the kids and they would want to run off into the bush and hide!

This Donaldson started off by painting a glowing picture of the scheme the Board had thought up for sending the young girls off to Cootamundra Girls' Home and convinced the people they should give it a chance. They sent a good few of them off, too, before we woke up to what was happening. One of the little girls, I remember, was little Maisy. She was the loveliest little thing. She was so looking forward to going to this wonderful place, because Donaldson had painted her such a marvellous picture of what it would be like. She never did see her mother again. She died in that Home and was buried there. They brought the police to take them by force sometimes, too.

They were supposed to be trained there — the girls to do housework, which they could learn at home anyway, and then they were sent out to work — as servants! The Board called it an 'apprenticeship system'. The employer was supposed to feed and clothe them, give them a very small bit of pocket money and the rest of their pay went to the Board to be paid to them when and if the Board decided. They couldn't go back home either, unless the Board told them. Many never saw their homes again.

A Kempsey man, George Davis, was the first one to organise the people around here to do something about this. A few of them went to see this Inspector about taking the children away but they were told that it didn't matter if the mothers cried buckets of tears, the children would still be taken; it was for their own good! It may have sounded like a good scheme but it was just cheap labour and so cruel. This 'apprentice system' was still going on even after they started to use the word 'assimilation' and stopped saying 'protection'.

I've told you about the Endowment, how they wouldn't give us the actual money, only a slip of paper. Well, the same thing happened with all of the other pensions as they were introduced. I even had to fight to get my grandmother the dole when I came back during the Depression. I had to go all the way up to the police station to collect it but it meant that I could get her some proper invalid's food and give her a bit of variety instead of our set ration that was decided for us. There was no choice with that and it was only about half as much as the dole. The same thing happened with the Old Age and Invalid Pensions which were *not* to be given to people living on the reserves — but we couldn't get off the reserves and we had nowhere else much to go if we could. I've had a look at some of these old records in the library in Sydney and it still hurts even to read them. It wasn't only in New South Wales either as the Federal Government took over pensions.

Some of these people were trying to help us, but how would you like to be treated like that? Do you wonder, then, at the demand for rights and looking after our own money? I'm not talking about so very long ago here, either, as changing from the Protection Board to the Welfare Board during the last war didn't make any difference. The big changes have only been in about the last ten years.

I hear and read all the criticism about money being given to Aborigines but this is what happened during my lifetime and now I can actually spend *all* of my Old Age Pension as I like. I know there are a lot of selfish people who are abusing the privileges my generation had to fight for but that's not because they are Aboriginal. I know too much of what it means to be an Aboriginal. Oh no, that's because they are people. There are enough who are bettering themselves and working in a selfless way but somehow they don't get mentioned as much.

I can tell you, I had a few fights with the Board about this sort of thing over the years. The first time was when I was working in Sydney and a cousin of mine came to work there too. The Board had agreed she could do so on the basis that her mother bought her some clothes and the lady she worked with added to them as part of her wage. But she didn't. One day, a policeman saw my cousin shopping for that woman without any shoes on her feet. He made some inquiries, and it came out that the Board didn't seem to care about what type of family it was they sent our girls to work for. Nor did they ever bother to check up to see that the agreements were being kept to.

100

Finally the Board sent her to work in a home where she wasn't paid wages for nine years! The money — 1s 6d a week and 5s a week after four years! — was supposed to be paid into the Board which 'minded' it for her. That was a laugh. So I went in with her to the Board to get the money that she had worked for all those years. Not only did they refuse to give her any, they also told me I was too light-skinned for them to help. I got that bit of information for nothing!

Anyway, I managed to get her a job with friends of the family I was working for then. They paid her twenty-five shillings a week — a lot of money those days. So we had a small victory there. Yes, that was the first time. I shudder to think how many times I crossed swords with that Board after that. It was either lie down and take the humiliation they doled out or stand up as a human being and ask to be treated like one. You ran the risk of an 'expulsion order' from the reserves though — for 'insolence' — so many were afraid to say much or they could be deprived of their rations and were not allowed the dole.

Just before the system ended, a relative of mine was expelled. The Board had changed its name to the Welfare Board, but it was the same Board. Her husband was working on the new Housing Commission houses in the town. He saw that they had proper bathrooms and even kitchen sinks, which ours never had, not even the new ones. He'd thought all government housing was much the same until then. We didn't have electricity, paths or fences like those houses, either. We were paying quite a bit in rent, too. The last straw was when the police went through all the houses looking for someone. They didn't knock or ask or anything. They trampled all over his vegetable garden, too, because there was no fence to protect it. He was worried about his wife and kids. Well, he complained officially to the Board about this but he got nowhere. Then he told them he wouldn't pay any more rent until he did get somewhere. He'd always been regular with his rent until then. They kept at him about his rent and he just kept telling them he wanted a bath and a sink and a fence

101

for a bit of privacy; then he'd have something worth paying rent for!

So he was to be evicted, given an 'expulsion order'. Other people owed rent; some never paid. But he'd been 'insolent'. Well, he decided to take it to court. The people from the unions in Newcastle helped him fight; the Newcastle Trades Hall set up a committee. I didn't like all this, but he said they were the only ones who'd offered any help. Nobody else did, and courts cost money. He was very upset later when the paper wrote it up as if he was being helped by communists. So was I. But he asked for help and no other organisation was interested. With their help he won the case, but then the Board tried again. They couldn't be beaten. In the second case he was made out as just a defaulter, and he lost. Before he could do anything else, he was evicted with all his kids. They had to live in a condemned house out of town. His wife spent the first few weeks scrubbing it down.

This frightened us all. It was meant to frighten us. We didn't know what to do. That was the way the Board always treated anyone who wouldn't just take whatever was done to them without complaining.

He's made good, though. He started his own fishing business and nearly starved himself to save up the deposit to buy his own home. He had to because the Board had made him out to be someone who wouldn't pay his rent. I think I understand better what he was trying to do now. When I was evicted, I had no organisation to fight for me, either, so what is the right way to do things? Anyway, that was the kind of 'protection' and 'welfare' we got!

One of the full-bloods on Purfleet I'll never forget was old Granny Sally. She was so old! The only piece of clothing she ever wore was an old petticoat wrapped around her shoulders and her arms stuck through the placket hole. Believe it or not, she used to teach the children to swim. They all had their duties to teach the children something and hers was to teach them to swim. What she'd do was simply throw you into the water and you had to swim or nearly drown. You read about that happening, but I can tell you that was the way old Granny Sally used to teach us. You soon learnt, too! Then she'd take all the bother of showing you *how*. What she did was a stroke that she used to call a 'bogey'. Actually it was much the same as the thing they call the butterfly stroke today.

There was one old Aboriginal we used to call Charlie. I saw him catch a goanna by just climbing the tree after it and grabbing it by the tail. Then he broke its back by cracking it around his head like a whip. I saw him do the same thing to a black snake. It was sliding into its hole as fast as it could go, when he grabbed it by the tail and cracked its back in the same way. The old people would often cook things like this that they would catch and offer some to us. We didn't often take up the invitations!

I saw the old full-bloods snare possums in a way that did not spoil the pelts. They always knew where the possums lived and used to set snares up against the right trees. Then they'd scatter cabbage tree tops around for the possums to eat. I've told you how they used to take the pelts into a shop in Tinonee where they had them weighed and put on a boat for Sydney. With the money they got for the pelts they would buy food from this shop and go back into the bush to snare more possums. They also sold koala bear skins there, too. I can remember one old fellow buying an old-fashioned gramophone with a big funnel on it. He carried it around in the bush wherever he went. You could hear this music coming towards you. Oh, he gave everybody a lot of laughs, lugging this gramophone all around the bush.

There was a borra, or what we call a corroboree, ground near Purfleet called Gillawarra. That's how we got the name of the gift shop, of course. Two creeks met at Gillawarra. One was fresh and the other was salty. They used the fresh water for drinking and speared fish in the salt water — it was a natural choice for a camp.

Old T. D. Trotter, who lived to be nearly a hundred, told me of the big corroborees they had there when he was a boy. He used to help them build up their fires and think it was a great privilege. They were very fond of this little white boy and he was very fond of them. He wanted so much to actually see them dance, but they always started well after he had been called home. He told me that one day he helped them when they built a canoe out of a tree. They hollowed it out and then blocked up each end. He was even allowed to help them try it out, he said. An old fullblood man and his wife took him out to catch fish. Not only was it quite stable, but they also cooked the fish there in the canoe itself! He tried some, but it was a bit too raw for him, he said, and they never used salt or anything like that.

As children, we were never allowed to go near the borra ground. It was a private thing between the men. There is only one part of an initiation ceremony when a woman takes part and that is when her son comes home after being initiated. Then, the mother is allowed to stand on one side with her face covered while her boy says his last farewell to her before leaving to go to his wife. The mother has to just stand there. The boy comes over and lays his head on her breast and puts his mouth to her nipple. That is the parting gesture; it is the last time he is allowed to touch his mother.

I do wish people would find out more about the Aboriginal way before they accuse them of being lazy or going 'walkabout' just when they feel like it or the many other wrong ideas about the tribal way. Some are even saying they were spirit worshippers which they were not, not in this southern part. They didn't worship spirits. How could you call them lazy when they had to work so hard to stay alive, hollow out a log with a stone axe, make all their own implements which had to be perfect? The only 'walkabout' in these parts was to follow the seasons; as the fish became scarce, they'd move away from the coast into the hills to spear animals and find berries and fruit. There's no aimless wandering there.

Oh yes, they were very strict about their marriage laws.

I've often told young people just how strict they were not so long ago. I once gave a talk on the subject. It was at a wedding and by the time I had finished telling them what used to be the situation regarding marriage, there was a very obvious silence around me.

I've often been asked about Aborigines marrying whites, as well, and I've got some funny reactions from people for telling them what I think. I've always been opposed to the people marrying outside their own kind, probably because of my own experiences in both worlds. My husband was even more opposed to it than I was or am. You know, it often seems to me that white people think we go and encourage our young people to marry whites because it is a step up for them. But it's quite the opposite. It just goes to show how many people totally misunderstand about the Aboriginal and his laws. But then again, I must admit I've had to change my opinions a lot, since I've recently seen some very happy marriages. The young people on both sides seem to accept more than my generation did. Basically I've come down to thinking that a marriage will last only if the couple love one another enough to withstand the pressures of the prejudices they are going to experience. Those prejudices are still just as strong as they were in many ways, and therefore the pressures are just as heavy as they used to be. The great trouble is, when you're advising young people whether to go ahead or not, is how do you find out beforehand that they are in fact going to love one another strongly enough? It's such a difficult situation to be in. All you can really do is say what you think and pray for their happiness.

Marriages were made by the elders of the tribe and they saw to it that they lasted, too. No man dared even look at a girl who had been chosen for a man who was away being initiated, for example. He could be away being initiated either as a 'Dalki', which is like being a part-time student I suppose, or a 'Keeparra', a full-time upholder of the law and customs. A Keeparra could be away as much as three years. When he came back, he knew all the tribe's laws and was made an elder. It was a great honour. His job was to help give the law, help people with

105

their problems, and punish anyone who broke the law. It was like being priest, judge and policeman.

Some of these people you hear about who are trying to get back to the traditional ways of the old people just don't seem to recognise just how strict the law was. They'd soon have a Keeparra after them with his bundi! Some of what they're doing and saying isn't even Aboriginal; it's come from outside or it's just made up.

There were also strict laws about marrying outside your particular tribe. Our tribe was called the Opossum tribe and my husband came from the Dingo tribe. These were the names of our particular crests or totems and we weren't allowed to eat or touch the thing the tribe was named after. A university professor recently asked me about these taboos. He was studying how tribal laws helped to keep the food supply from running out. He called it 'conservation' and 'ecology', of course! Anyway, I was told by my father-in-law-to-be that I was just not allowed to marry anyone from the Dingo tribe. But we got over that by having a Christian marriage instead of a tribal one, and we couldn't have been happier together. I didn't think twice about it. I've always seemed to belong to both worlds.

Some of the legends we used to be taught obviously were designed to make us keep the law or just be better people. They had to be treated very seriously indeed, you know. One of them was the legend about the small muckarung, or lizard, which was once a young Aboriginal woman who had disobeyed the law and gone near a borra ground. She was punished by being turned into a muckarung which sits on a log waving its front legs, just as if it was signalling, 'Go back, go back!!'

There is also a small spider — very flat and very black. The legend goes that this small spider was once a young man who was having an affair with a married woman. The tribe caught him out and, with their bundis, they flattened him so that he turned into this spider. The story of the echidna is very similar. A member of a hunting party used to remain behind and go to the camp where the young girls stayed while everybody else was out getting food. There were never any footprints to prove that he had been there, yet the tribe suspected him. So one time one of the men stayed behind to watch him. He saw the young man climb a very young tree which then bent over with his weight and dropped him neatly in the middle of the girls' camp. The other men were called and they came back with their spears to punish him. Now, the usual punishment gave the man who was to be punished a chance to dodge the spears if he could. But this young man just ran away. When they caught up with him, he lay on the ground hiding his head, so the tribe threw their spears into his back and that's how the echidna got all its spikes.

Here's another one I remember: The scrub turkey was a very lazy bird and very jealous of all the other birds that had brightly-coloured feathers and were always flying busily around the place. One day he stole a fire stick from a camp fire and set the bush alight. It was the worst bushfire that ever was. The birds were terrified and flew into the sea and that's why we have got so many wonderfully-coloured fish. But the scrub turkey finished up a dirty brown colour with a bright red comb. The comb, you see, was the fire stick on his head. That was his punishment for being so jealous and doing such a horrible thing.

Oh yes, the old Aborigines had a way of putting fear into the children to stop them from wandering off and getting lost. They told them about the 'Goi-on'. Now, if you asked an Aboriginal child what the Goi-on was like, one might say it was white, another might say it was black or pink. One might say it was tall or it was short. It all depended. It was all sorts of things to different children, because it was just a device that the older people used to scare them a little. Something like a ghost. When I had charge of the shop, a man from up north came and tried to sell me a clay model to put in the shop. He said it was a Goi-on, but I knew better. I wouldn't have it. The Aborigines have never liked images around these parts and, anyway, there was no one form that was a Goi-on.

I must tell you that, later on, you only had to say to a child, 'There's a white man over there!' and they'd come running back to you. The white man took the place of the Goi-on in stopping children from running off and getting lost, you see. I have to admit that I used that one a few times myself because it really worked!

I used to spend a lot of time with these tribal people wandering around the bush. They showed me the things that you could eat out there and the things that were poisonous, and also what you could use for medicine. They watched the birds before they'd try to eat a new berry or fruit, for example. And there used to be a lot of wild fruits you could eat with perfect safety out in the bush; there were the raspberries, yams, the wild grapes, the fruit of the Lilly-pilly which the possums loved, the apple berries which we called 'puddings' and which we chewed because they were supposed to be good for general health . . . all sorts of things. And all sorts of things that you couldn't eat, either. There were others that were good for specific illnesses. The fruit of the native cherry, which is very bitter, was chewed for indigestion, especially by pregnant women. They never used salt with their food, but they did sometimes drink sea water for their health. They used to boil the leaves of the native raspberries, too, for stomach complaints.

Then there was what they called the 'snake herb' because goannas used to eat it after being attacked by snakes. It was crushed and put on bruises and the like. They used to also crush the leaves of the Cunjevoi and apply it to stings or use it on festering sores or boils. The rough side was put on and left for a couple of days to draw the pus out and then the smooth side was bashed and applied to help the healing. I can remember my grandmother using it on women with ulcers on the breasts with very good results.

If an ant stung a child, they would place a stick across the bite and tap it with another stick very gently until the

108

pain went away. Bloodwood gum was crushed into a ball, put in boiling water, and the liquid drunk for diarrhoea. A particular wattle bark was bruised, put into hot water and drunk for drying up the lungs and also to stop any looseness in the bowels. The nut of the Geebung was chewed, as was charcoal, for teeth and for indigestion. And even the pure white ash from the eucalyptus and the tea tree was put aside for use on wounds or after circumcision in the initiation ceremonies, or during childbirth. Oh yes, the old people weren't stupid; they'd had thousands of years of trying out remedies. They probably knew more about medicines than the white man did when he arrived in this country. These are only a few of the ones I have experienced.

Gran was very clever at nursing people by using the information she had got from these people. Of course, as I've told you, she had also been carefully taught by the white family who had reared her. I used to go around with her a lot and she talked to me about the medical knowledge she'd learned from the tribal people. She could always make do with what she had or had to go out and find for herself. If she ran out of proper medicines, she could always do something for some poor person in pain. That's why she was so good and so respected for what she did.

I remember her telling me how one of the old women had taken her into her confidence one day and had told her what she had to do to bring her baby into the world. They worked out the months by the moon, as they worked out the time of day by the sun.

She was not allowed to show herself to the men with this big 'binji'. They built her a leaf or bark camp back-to-back with her mother's camp. Then she had to prepare the white ash to be used as an antiseptic, then the special stones they used for cutting the navel cord, and finally the clean bark for applying the ash to the wound. Aboriginal babies were born with their mothers on their knees so that the baby wouldn't smother and also so that the mother could see that everything was all right with the baby as it came out. They led such an active life, you see, that usually they didn't have much trouble with their births.

The mother had to bury the afterbirth because they believed that it could be dried, crushed, and mixed with eucalyptus leaves to hide it and used as a poison by putting it in drink or food, and it couldn't be detected. They really believed that, but, even if they didn't, you can see why it was good to bury it anyway.

The last of the full-bloods were Kate and Florrie, the daughters of Albert Lobban. I went to school with them. They were some of the ones sent down to our school from up past Gloucester. I never knew how old they were. They were older than the rest of us but they never bothered about birthdays. Kate was brilliant at all her school work. She could also play any musical instrument perfectly, and she and her sister sang so sweetly. They sang the different parts in a choir the missionaries trained.

They were taken down to Sydney to sing. There was a big gathering in Sydney straight after the Jubilee Singers were out from America, and one of the missionaries took them down to it. Kate was to lead the alto part in this special singing group which was to follow on from these American singers. They were a great success and had a wonderful time, except for the colour bar. They couldn't stay at some places where they wanted to stay because of the colour of their skin. They often spoke of that. I particularly remember that visit because they went down by boat and that boat was wrecked at the river mouth the trip after they returned!

They married and stayed down on the coast. Kate was Mrs Tom Davis and Florrie was Mrs Stan Carter. They played a very active part in our lives. They were wonderful women. They knew so much about the bush and about Aboriginal culture. They hardly ever mixed with white people and usually spoke their own language. They taught me so much.

I was in hospital when Kate and Florrie were both in there very sick. Florrie had TB and so was in a different part of the hospital from Kate. (Aborigines weren't allowed

into the main part, of course. For most of my life, being in
hospital meant being tucked away in the isolation wards
out the back, or stuck on an open verandah. They must
have thought colour was contagious! All that has changed
now, thank goodness.) Anyway, this day everything was
quiet. Then suddenly there was the sound of pathetic
wailing from somewhere in the hospital. Kate heard of
Florrie's death and was showing her grief for her sister
with the Aboriginal death wail. It was such a sad sound. I
remember Matron Everingham was so touched by it that
she put her arms around Kate and tried to comfort her.
The date was 27 April 1956.

Not too long after that, Kate died from cancer of the
face. She had agreed to go to Sydney for ray treatment.
She had never been further than the hospital verandah
before that and so she was terrified by the ray room. They
couldn't give her the full ray treatment so she was sent
back again and I ended up looking after her. She died
such a terrible death. It was 31 March 1964. And so they
had finally gone, the last of the full-bloods.

Quite a few Aboriginal people used to camp at Saltwater
during Christmas. I remember going there often with my
in-laws. Not many people went there then. There was no
fresh water—or so they thought! We had plenty. The men
knew exactly where to dig. They dug deep holes and only
had to wait a little while before fresh water seeped through
the sand and into their holes. They certainly got enough
to keep us all going—for drinking, washing, cooking and
all that.

This was also my first experience of staying in one of
their camps made from the bark of the tea tree. It has the
most wonderful bark that comes off in great sheets. It's no
wonder we call it the paperbark tree. My husband and
another man selected their trees and then marked out
their bark. They'd then make a W-shaped cut at the top
and a straight cut at the bottom, and hit the bark with the
blunt part of their axe to loosen it. A sharp cut down the

111

tree and they could peel the bark off. It came off in a round ring. To straighten it, they lit a fire and put the bark ring around it until it was warm. They could then flatten it out without cracking it at all. They weighted it down on a flat piece of land while they went to another tree.

They cut a lot of poles to make the rafters and the frame. These they tied to a firm, well-established tree that wouldn't move in the wind. The bark then went on just as though they were making an iron roof, up and down, no cracks, no dints, nothing that would leak. They were warm, dry and cosy little huts.

One time we were down there it was very wet. Heavy coastal rain. The whole camp was quite dry because they used what they called a galley. It was a sort of canopy that stretched out from the camp to the fire. You could go back and forth from the camp to the fire to do your cooking and not be disturbed by the wet. I was very impressed by the cleverness of that, you know.

Oh, and then there was Jess and her baby. Jess was a young unmarried mother and the time had come for her baby. It was the first time for her. The trouble was she was a deaf mute and I couldn't communicate with her because I didn't know sign language.

Well, I was called out in the middle of the night for her. As I came in sight of the hut, I saw that they had a big fire burning outside and this was giving a lot of light. There was Jess standing up by that fire with her legs crossed! I hurried up to her and tried to make her lie down, but she refused to. I quickly made a bed in front of the fire and then tried to make her lie down on that. Still she refused. She was standing there like that, waiting until the ambulance came.

I knew how long it would take to cross the river on the punt. I could see that the ambulance would never arrive there on time, let alone get her into hospital. And then I realised what she was trying to do. She was deliberately stopping the birth of the child by standing up and crossing

112

her legs! I knew that that would only do damage to her and to the baby, so I got rough with her and forced her to lie down on the bed. I got her into position and the baby came straight away.

I still remember vividly the little heads that were peeping out from inside the hut. There were about three or four little kiddies having a real eyeful of what was going on. Anyway I got the baby and sorted out everything before the ambulance arrived. I can tell you that I breathed a sigh of relief when I saw it swing into the reserve. It turned out that little Jess had hurt herself inside and had to have a few stitches, but other than that everything turned out all right.

The child was a girl. Her mother called her Fay and she turned out a lovely person. But she never did get to know what a time she gave me!

Yes, the old full-blood people have long since gone from around here. And when I think of them my mind goes back to poor Dave Sands's funeral. As I looked at his poor widow and the children I wondered why God had taken young Dave away, just when he was on the very threshold of possibly getting the world championship — at the very height of his brilliant career. Why such a *silly* accident happening to our Dave who had not only got himself fame, but had brought so much self-respect and dignity to his people ... those people who had never experienced much of those two things in the white man's world. I don't know. Some day we'll understand, I suppose.

11

NO WONDER WE STILL CALL THEM FRINGE DWELLERS

My father-in-law was a very gracious old gentleman. He was a full-blood, initiated man; a real Keeparra who knew and respected the old laws and expected others to live by them. He was born at the head of the Wallamba River at a place called Coomba so the people called him 'Coomba George'.

In the early days of his marriage he was deserted by his wife. He was left with six boys and a girl to cope with. He not only did cope, but he kept them all together. When the two older ones got married their wives helped out with the younger ones in the family, and so on.

Coomba George was a fisherman. He was always after the big jewfish. He made his own nets out of rope which he had sent up from the Chinese markets in Sydney. He'd take days to plait a net that was suitable for him. He went about it in true Keeparra fashion. He sat there preparing everything just right before he went fishing.

Actually his wife came back years later and he forgave her. They never lived together again, but he was always kind and sympathetic towards her.

My husband was very much like his father. He took his mother in to live with us, even though most of the family hadn't forgiven her. The poor thing, she had taken ill

114

after the birth of the twin boys, who were the youngest. She started having epileptic fits. That might have been prevented had there not been such a lack of adequate nursing in those days.

The first fit hit her while they were out in the boat fishing. She was nursing one of the boys when all of a sudden she took a fit and jerked the baby off her lap and into the water. Coomba George fortunately had the presence of mind to dive in and save him. If it hadn't been for the long dresses all babies wore in those days he would have drowned. It kept it afloat just for that little while, you see.

My mother-in-law died at our place. There was a bad storm that night and I thought I heard a groan in the early hours of the morning, but put it down to the weather. Next morning, when I went to take in her early morning cup of tea before I went to work, I found the poor thing dead. I told my sons the storm had taken her. You know, as I looked at her pale face, I thought to myself that she was now free to go to her people and free from the fits and complaints that come to old people. She had been like me — she had had a white father and had been brought up in the bush. I knew only too well what she had gone through as a half-caste. It was unforgivable leaving her young family like that and running off, I know. But I instinctively knew what kinds of strains she had had to face throughout her life.

Old Coomba George used to stay with us when his wife wasn't there. He played the violin. That might seem unusual, but most of the men played the violin then. My boys used to always ask him to play the violin for them. There was one particular favourite tune of his that he used to play so sweetly . . . and all the time. One day we asked him the name of it. He said it was called 'The Wind Swept the Barley'! It must have been a hit tune once upon a time, but heavens, that must have been a long time ago! Oh, we had a few laughs about it as well.

115

Coomba George grew up with my grandfather and his two brothers. That was at the Wallamba. In those days, Coomba was an Aboriginal camping ground. There were only a few people living between there and Forster then, which goes to show how things have shot ahead. It was all bush those days. I can still recall walking through that area a long time ago. No, not so long, either. The bush was so thick that you got scratched and your clothes got torn. You walk through all that housing development now and you can hardly credit it.

There were some really lovely places around here when it was all mostly bush. Near Hawke Head my husband and his brother used to dive for lobsters in a small cave they knew. They turned them over and put them in a tin with salt water. We'd be waiting up on the hill with a fire all ready. I don't think I'll ever see again catches of lobsters like they used to get, now that civilisation has overrun the place.

Actually it took me a while to get used to eating lobsters and other salt water things like that. I'd been a 'drylander' all my life and my husband had always lived by the sea. The first time I tasted lobster was when I went out with him to meet his father and family. They gave me some as well as some oysters. After I'd eaten them I had a bilious attack! His brother told me a way I could get used to them and that was to soak them in fresh water first and then eat them with vinegar, salt and pepper. Even then I could only take them with lots of bread and butter!

This same visit, my husband took me in a boat up the lake. I was amazed at how he could stand up in that little boat without rolling it over, see the fish and then spear them with only one throw. That was really something to see. He showed me how to spot the fish but, soon after we were married, the authorities banned the Aborigines from fishing with a spear. They reckoned they were taking too many fish. Yet how about all the spearfishermen you see today! Anyway, I never did get to try standing up in that little boat and throwing a spear at fish. That was a great shame.

When I decided to get married I didn't have a church wedding. We were married at a Registry Office. Nobody worried about me in those days very much. I was a loner. I had no reception and no honeymoon. In fact I even had a couple of witnesses that I had never met before! I got just one wedding present and that was a tea set. At least it was something that came in handy.

Oh, my husband and I had our ups and downs just like every other couple, but we stuck it out. We used to talk things over and put our trust in each other, no matter what. I think that that is the secret of a happy married life — to love and trust one another. My husband was always talking about that and he reckoned that if one partner went wrong, the other partner would always find out in some way or another, because you just can't hide secrets for too long without letting something slip. We had our odd skeleton in the cupboard, I wouldn't deny that. Irrespective of who or what we are, we all have them.

Anyway, after we had decided to marry, his mother did invite us to go and live with them but as I had no family it would have been a one-sided affair. So we went to live in a condemned house instead! It was so unsafe that nobody else would go into it. When the wind blew, the whole place would rattle. But it was good enough for us at the time — anything was, I can tell you! — until we had built our own place.

My husband worked and so did I. We bought the timber from the mill for our first home and set up a tent where we planned to build. We did try to get our own piece of land, but it turned out to be on what they called Water Board land. It was outside of the reserve at Purfleet, but we wanted to live there because it was near the water and we so much wanted to have our own fowls and garden and all that.

Well, the Protection Board saw us endeavouring to build our home and to our amazement they had all the iron we needed sent up from Sydney! It turned out a three-bed-room house with a verandah all around it. We got our garden and it was lovely. It became a show place for the area. Whenever the manager had friends over or visitors, he would bring them out to see it. Oh, that was one thing all those Managers knew ... that Ella Simon had a clean house and a nice garden that they could show off!

Strictly speaking we should have gone to live at Forster because my husband was born and bred there. The trouble was I didn't like Forster one little bit. For one thing I didn't like the wind that blew there every day or the black sand. When you went to bed at night there, your feet would be filthy because of that black sand that was everywhere. Black sand, sand, sand ... even in your food. I was a bit bronchial, too, and that didn't make me feel any fonder of that sea wind blowing all the time.

Just before the war broke out we had a terrible drought. Everything was tinder dry and there were bushfires all over the place. Everybody was having such a bad time of it that jobs were terribly difficult to get.

The Manager had to get tanks of water sent in from Taree. Each one of us could only get a few pots of water a day. You couldn't wash in it; there was precious little of it to do anything with. In fact, that tank didn't hold anywhere near enough water for our needs. We still had to do our own searching for water.

There was a place called Carles Creek about a mile or so away from Purfleet and we had to carry water from there. Blue Well also had clean enough water. And if we couldn't get a drop from out of those, there was always the old dam where we did our washing. But we soon found out this was stagnant because the kiddies started to get sores. These weren't helped, either, by the scarcity of green vegetables we all had in our diets.

Oh, those days were hard. With not enough fresh vegetables and very little fresh water, our children were really starting to get sick. My husband and my uncle had to go away in search of work. But it seemed that jobs, too, had dried up. Three of our boys were still going to school and they did get a small ration each, but that still wasn't enough. I cooked my own bread, of course, and worked while my husband was away looking for something to do. He was getting so crestfallen about it all! Anyway, he finally managed to get a job on a farm right away down at Avoca, and even that didn't last long. By now we were starting to get really desperate. But for me, a worse blow was to come.

The day came when war broke out, and he left immediately to enlist. He was so proud of himself.

We all had no doubts that he'd be taken into the army. There was no discrimination about that. None of us ever dreamed he would be turned down. He was young enough, and big and strong, that was for sure. But, next thing I know he was returning home. I went out to meet him and then saw the disappointment in his face. I didn't have to ask him the result of his check-up.

He had known the doctor because they used to go out fishing together. He just told him, 'Well, Joe, you can go home and fish as much as you like. I don't think you'll ever be able to join the army.'

That didn't satisfy me. I just couldn't bring myself to think even for a moment that my husband was that ill. We went down to Newcastle to see a specialist. The news was even worse than I could have possibly guessed. My Joe had hardening of the arteries and high blood pressure. And yet here was a man who still played football, coached a team of youngsters, and even ran miles each morning just to keep fit.

He finally decided that his war work could be back down on the farm at Avoca where he had been working. The farmer had got a contract for growing vegetables for the army, and we had to work hard to keep up the supplies. Instead of there not being any jobs for miles around, now suddenly labour was scarce everywhere. We had to train youngsters to pick the vegetables. But at least now we had plenty of vegetables to go on with, but the coupons never seemed to go far enough for such things as tea, butter and meat for a family with three growing boys. Fortunately, my sister-in-law worked in a factory and could buy surplus coupons for a few shillings. I know this was part of the so-called Black Market but we were desperate with these three boys to feed and clothe, like so many other families. If it wasn't for those extra coupons, all our basic diet would have been vegetables and mutton. Then, if we were lucky, we might catch a few fish or collect a few abalones.

It was hard work for me. I used to do most of the packing. We had to be up at four in the morning to have the vegetables all ready for the lorry to pick up at four that afternoon. There was no waiting. If you weren't ready, the lorry would drive on. There weren't many lorries available.

The army expected the best quality vegetables, too, so they had to be looked after at every stage in their growth. The boss had a knack for growing early season vegetables. He'd put a packet of cucumber seeds in a wet corn bag and leave it on a rack beside the fuel stove. The heat would germinate the seeds while the men prepared the soil and made the small mounds to plant the seeds. When the tendrils appeared in the seeds, I'd have to carefully take each seed out and plant it. It was my job to look after these young plants as it was delicate work and my hands were smaller than the men's.

After a day's work, I used to be ready for bed, all right. But it wasn't over then. I'd have to cook for the family. One of the hardest things about that wasn't so much actually doing it, but trying to think how I could cook the same old thing in a different way from the day before!

One hot day, towards the end of the season when things were starting to slacken off and the boys had gone down for a swim, a big bushfire came racing towards the old farmhouse where we were living. Everything was still tinder dry from the drought and there was a vicious wind behind the fire. We had only a tiny bit of water left in the tanks and only the boss, his wife, Joe and myself were there to fight the fire. I raced inside and put our clothes and blankets in the bath and covered them with bags that we used to use to cover the windows during blackouts. If the worst came to the worst I was going to turn the tap on. What I was most worried about was that we didn't have any coupons left to buy new clothes.

120

Anyway, that fire just came on and on. Suddenly I was overcome by smoke, and coughing and spluttering everywhere. My husband yelled out to me to lie down and cover my face. There was nothing else I could do. I can tell you that, as I lay there, I prayed like I've never prayed before or after. Then, just as suddenly as it had blown our way in the first place, the fire was blown back on itself by a wind change. We were out of danger.

The boss's wife and I used to talk about that terrible day and, no matter how much we discussed it, it still seemed a miracle. If it wasn't a miracle, it was the nearest thing to one.

I used to have to go to Sydney and pick up the cheques for the boss. The train used to get me in there very early and I'd have breakfast at the station. You were lucky if you could get a proper meal, but there was one morning that I remember very well indeed, because they had lamb's fry and bacon! Now, during the war, anything that was a change in food was a real highlight of your day. I sat down opposite a soldier and he and I both ordered the same thing. His came first. On the plate was a lovely big piece of bacon. My mouth was really watering.

But when mine came ... no bacon! So I asked the waitress why and was told quicksmart that the man was a soldier and could have anything he wanted, but I had to take what came and that was all there was to it. I remember being sorely tempted to say that I was working my fingers to the bone to feed fresh vegetables to men like him while I couldn't get a decent feed myself, but then I made myself think about it. He deserved it. He was probably going off to war. It's funny how you remember little things like that.

Well, when the war ended, the demand for vegetables wasn't so great, of course. Anyhow, Joe and I, we were both so tired that we were starting to get on each other's nerves. Oh, that meant we must have been tired, I can tell you! I just wanted to go home, job or no job, so we finally told the boss that that was what we were going to do. He wasn't too pleased about it, but quite frankly that didn't matter to us by now. So we packed up and went home.

121

Back at Purfleet we found our house had been broken into and a great deal of our things all destroyed. But at least I was home again!

With the bit of money we had managed to save up during that time, Joe was able to buy sufficient gear to go back to fishing. It was what he had wanted to get back to and he figured that, with the boys helping out, he could make a real go of it. The trouble was that the boys, just like a lot of sons, weren't interested in doing what their father wanted them to do. By now they had grown up enough to have their own firm ideas on what they wanted to do with their lives. Well, at least they had firm ideas on what they *didn't* want to do — and that was be fishermen. Even when my Joe did manage to get them to go out with him, there were always quarrels, which was to be expected.

Joe just wasn't up to doing all that hard work on his own, and it was hard work, I can tell you. Besides, fish weren't plentiful then for some reason and his health hadn't been improved by working so hard down on the vegetable farm during the war. So finally he brought the boat in and started to use it for prawning in the river. I'd help him after work to wash and cook them, but I couldn't really give him all the help he needed. And then, sometimes, somebody would steal our nets off the racks. Things were just going wrong generally. Oh, there were some good days with really good catches, but for every good day, there was more than one bad day. Still, we managed to carry on with it for a few years, but, poor Joe, he was soon in for a bitter disappointment.

For the first time in our whole marriage, he didn't discuss something with me before going into it. One day he was working on his own, the next he had gone into partnership with a white person. They decided that they would buy all the fishing gear needed to get out where the big catches were to be had and they would go halves. I wasn't very happy about the whole thing from the start. This person knew nothing about fishing, and I just

122

somehow knew he was all talk and no action. What made it worse was that he wanted to make the decision about when they should go out and when they shouldn't. My husband would tell him that such and such a time wasn't the right time. He used to try to tell him that there was a certain time, a certain place, certain things to do before you could catch certain fish and all that. But this man just wouldn't be told. He even had the nerve to accuse my Joe of being lazy! Or, if Joe did just shrug his shoulders and go out when he was told, this person would fly off into a rage because they hadn't caught any fish. It got so unbearable that finally I had to step in and tell my husband that I thought the best thing to do was to give him away. And that's what he did.

But it turned out that we were the losers, not that other person. He sold the boat but only got the deposit on it because the new owner slept in it one night and just left it there on the side of the river. Sure enough, a flood came and washed it away. So after all those war years of hard work, of saving to do something that we had hoped would give us something to live on . . . it had all been washed away. It was the first and last time my Joe and I ever pulled in different directions and it turned out disastrously.

We went out west next. The car we had was totally useless and would never have got us there. So we sold it for scrap and bought an old Chevrolet truck. You know, that old truck proved to be worth its weight in gold. It even survived a visit to the bottom of the river at Forster!

What happened was that we had gone out to Forster for our Christmas holidays and had that old thing packed brimful with our bedding, gifts and food. We were first on the punt, which has now been replaced by the bridge, thank goodness. A bus came on behind us and the first thing I knew was that we were rolling forward. The gates weren't fastened properly, either, so we just went happily straight through them and on into the river. One of our boys was nursing a kiddy and he had sense enough to

smash in the side window as we went down. They just shot
to the surface. My husband's door opened, too, and he also
shot straight up. But I was sitting in the middle and I just
went down with the ship!

Suddenly I found myself being lifted up by something
and being shot to the top long after everybody else. They
said later that it must have been an air pocket in the cabin.
I don't know about that, but I've never been more thankful
for anything, air pocket or no air pocket.

Anyway, Joe stayed with the truck and we went home,
dripping wet, in the bus. Do you know, on the very next
day he arrived home driving that silly truck, not in the least
any the worse for its bath!

The newspapers, of course, made a big thing out of it.
A reporter asked me what I had valued most out of what
I had lost. I knew what that was straight away. It was my
old bible. It had gone floating out to sea. So, all round,
it wasn't the best of Christmases, that one wasn't.

Oh yes, there were good days and there were bad days.
It's all changed now. You know, I often sit here and think
how sad it all is, really. I think of the black man who once
owned the land, wandered through the bush making his
own way . . . finding his own water holes, his food, cooking
it on his own fire . . . and how happy he was in his own way
of living.

Now the Aboriginal has tasted alcohol — a different
kind of fire and water. His old cures are no match for the
new diseases and, afraid to go to doctors, he bears his pain
alone. His tribal law is all broken down, those same laws
that had meant so much to his forefathers.

Funnily enough, I did seem to notice that on the coast
the Aboriginal man was in some ways more readily accepted
by white society. He was a good footballer, runner, boxer,
horseman. He was always happy in sport of some kind or
another. You name it and he would be in it. The dark
man away out back, way out west, somehow didn't get
the same privileges. That's what I think anyway.

At least I can look over my seventy years and remember the joy that was there when we had our own dreamtime stories, roamed through the bush, learned the way of the legends, ate the fruits and the berries, and heard the birds talk to us. Aborigines are going through what is probably the severest test of their history, having to come from a stone age to an electronic one of space and rockets in so short a time. They can do it but it's no wonder they are living on the fringe of society. No wonder we still have to call them fringe dwellers.

12

SO MUCH HEARTACHE,
SO MUCH PAIN

In my day Aborigines weren't allowed in hotels or any other licensed place. They weren't even allowed to carry alcoholic drinks, let alone buy them. They couldn't have it on reserves and they couldn't have it in public places — which meant just about anywhere. They just couldn't have it.

This went on for many, many years. There was always someone getting caught or being reported. There was always some 'sympathetic' white man ready to buy his black 'pals' a drink or two, or sell it to them for a bit of profit, and this was the cause of a lot of the disturbances — the white man willing to give it to the black man if there was something in it for him. Oh, sure, the white man who did that might be given a big fine to pay. But the poor Aboriginal was always put in gaol. There was no fine or an 'or else' for him. And it usually meant at least one month in Maitland Gaol, over one hundred miles away.

Gaol sentences stopped nothing. Even with the 'big boss' Manager always there ready to stop booze coming in to the reserve. How could you really stop it, when all around white people were drinking, and drinking as much as they liked without being sent to gaol for it? The injustice was obvious.

126

Photographs of different types of graves in an old Aboriginal cemetery which is now closed

The fenced-off area is another kind of Aboriginal grave

ABOVE: Ella Simon, J.P.
BELOW: A picture theatre, with hard seats in the front for Aborigines. There was also a special door at the front through which they had to enter after the lights went out.
Photo 'The Good Old Days', Jim Revitt

The cave at Blackhead

You know, I personally believe that was how drinking of methylated spirits got a foothold. The people weren't able to drink liquor, but once they got the taste they wanted more just as much as so many white people do. It was easier to buy metho. It wasn't illegal and you didn't get thrown in gaol for drinking or carrying it, unless you were drunk. So a lot of the people started to drink this stuff and, of course, it made them just as drunk and stupid as it does anybody, whatever the colour of his skin.

It's really an insult to human intelligence to say that, when it comes to drinking, Aborigines are any different to anybody else. I've seen too much of life to believe that, seen too many drunk. I've worked in too many homes, been to too many parties and functions. It is true that people turn to drink as a way of escape from hopelessness and the Aboriginal is doing that — but so are the whites.

Anyway, they pretty soon got around to stopping *all* Aborigines buying metho at all. It didn't matter whether you wanted it around the home, or whether you wanted to use it for the purposes for which it was there on the shop shelves, oh no. You just weren't allowed to purchase it.

I had a primus stove at that time, because I used to work and didn't have time to light fires after working all day. So I made sure that little primus was always handy. Anyway one day I went down to the local shop to get a bottle of metho for it. They turned around and told me that I couldn't buy a bottle of metho at any price! They said I had to go and get a permit from the Manager to say it was all right with him for me to buy the stuff! Oh, this really got me mad. Here I was, a non-drinker, and a mother, and well known as a church worker, only wanting something to light my stove with! So I strode out of that shop and I went home and lit a wood fire. I wasn't going to ask anyone for a permit just to light a primus. I told them off, too! But, oh, there's been so many, many deaths caused by that horrible stuff. There were too many years of them having to sneak off into the bush with a bottle of it. It became a sort of 'sneaky craving' so that even changing the law to let Aborigines go into hotels didn't make any difference.

I think one of the saddest things that has happened with the drink is that the young men have started to get into it so soon in their lives. It was the same thing in the old days. They would wander off into town and try to find someone who would buy them a drink, or take their money and buy it for them.

So many terrible things happened because of this stupid law. It went on for so long. Even the men who'd been away at the war found that as soon as they were out of uniform they could no longer drink with their mates. Others had friends they worked with or played sport with who could drink freely, so why shouldn't they? So of course they'd go to any lengths just to buy a bottle of beer. They'd hang around town until they found someone who'd risk buying it for them. Then they'd have to hide while they drank it. They weren't even allowed to drink in the privacy of their own homes because they could be searched without warning.

I remember young Cecil Bungie got caught on this. He was such a nice young man. He was a good worker; worked for the same people for quite a while. They were very fond of him. He also helped one of the fishermen who thought the world of young Cecil. He had a dear old mother and father. The father had worked hard all his life as a gardener for many people in the town. They had other sons, but Cecil was a special favourite. He was so good to his parents; always ready to do the garden or anything else around the home.

Well, I don't know how, but in some way Cecil got introduced to the drink. One night he went over to town and got someone to buy him one bottle of beer. Now, I haven't mentioned it before, but another of the ways we were 'protected' was that the Managers had the power to impose a curfew on us, which they did. We weren't allowed over in the town after dark. So, under the Protection Act, Cecil was committing two crimes: it was after our curfew

128

time and he had this one bottle of beer under his coat. He was hurrying down a lane heading for the bridge when he saw the police turn the corner ahead of him. He was terrified. They would send him off to gaol if they found he had a bottle of beer. They chased him. He panicked. He ran down to the river and jumped in. He was a good swimmer, but he had his overcoat on; he had boots on; he was being chased; he was afraid.

That boy drowned. I'll never forget that.

His mother and father came to tell me that their son was missing; that he'd been seen in the water. I'll never forget their faces; so full of fear and grief. That father walked for days, all the way to the river and along the banks, back and forth across that bridge looking for his boy. There were people diving and fishermen rowing up and down the river looking for the body. The mother was beside herself. She was very frail and sick anyway. I went down every day to sit with her. We would talk about things. But she'd keep coming back to how good her son was to her; what she would miss about him; and the events of that awful night. The broken-hearted father would come home and he'd just keep saying that his boy would not have drowned if it wasn't for the fear of the police in his mind. He couldn't accept it.

They found the body, caught in some weeds on the bottom of the river. His poor mother broke down when they told her. She just screamed and screamed. I held her in my arms and tried to quieten her. There was nothing else I could do. You can't say to a mother or father, 'Try not to take any notice of the fact that you've both had your hearts broken'. What can you say? It was such a needless death. A lovely young life lost just because people didn't understand.

Most decent people, white and black, were very upset about Cecil's death. I say most, because I didn't notice much sympathy when the police came to tell his parents that he was missing. One of them said, 'Your boy is somewhere in that big drink'. Yet he was one of the men who had chased Cecil that night. I wonder whether it was

129

ever on his conscience. I'm sorry, but I just can't think it would have been.

And so it has been with much of the history of the Aborigines and the whites. So much heartache, so much pain, so much cruelty. And not enough on the conscience when there should have been.

13

SOMETHING WAS TOUCHING
THEIR CONSCIENCES

I've always had to have a 'tag'. I've found that if you go
along on your own bat you never count for anything in other
people's eyes; but if you have a label they can understand
easily why they should accept you. One of my labels or
tags has been a member of the United Aborigines' Mission.
And I don't mean 'tag' cynically. I've been very proud of
being a member of the Mission.

I was able to do such a lot more for Aboriginal people as
a Mission member. That wasn't only just in Purfleet,
either, but in a whole host of places — different people with
different problems and needing different kinds of help.
I don't mean only spiritual kinds of help.

The UAM is an interdenominational mission working
among Aborigines. The first thing that comes to my mind
when I think about our Mission was when four of us paid a
visit to Gerard. That's a reserve in South Australia.

Gerard was run by a missionary, who was also in the
Mission. With the small legacy he was left by his father he
had bought a lovely place right near the Murray River
and put some sheep on it. Then he built the reserve up
for the local black people. Oh, it was really well run and
I felt even at that time that he was really doing something
positive for the people. But the nagging trouble was, you

see, that he was still the 'white boss'. For example, he
ran the store himself and forebade the selling of tobacco.
I felt that that sort of thing was a great mistake. If the
people couldn't get, say, tobacco from him, then they were
going to wander off into town where they could get it freely.
And that was precisely the thing he didn't want them to
do, I expect, because he must have known that they'd
more than likely get a bit of drink while they were at it. Oh,
well.

They were mostly full-blooded people in the reserve at
Gerard. We were there for a month to try to show them
that there was a better way for the Aboriginal to live.
Anyway, when we arrived at the station the missionary was
there to pick us up. There was a truckload of the people
there, too. Oh, that was quite a picture. Some of them had
white dust coats on — at least they used to be white. There
was this red dust everywhere in that place and what between
that and the grease, they looked a pitiable sight.

We were taken to the missionary's home to brush up
and eat before the first of what became regular night
meetings with the people. Usually by the time they got
home from work, went to the store, had a meal, got spruced
up for the meeting, it would be almost ten-thirty to eleven
o'clock at night before we could finally get started. But,
after we had got started, we usually had a hard time in
getting them to go home!

As I said, there were four of us — two men and another
woman. We had to take the women's talks between us
two women. The object was to try and teach them hygiene
and so on. Oh, just not tell them about it, because a lot
of them had heard it all before, but why it made sense to
be hygienic. Our men would talk with any of the local men
who might come in. After that we would go to a place for
supper and get to bed well after midnight. This went on
night after night.

There was one particular young man I was interested
in trying to help. He was an odd one. He had run away from
his tribal area to marry a girl of his own choice. She had
been given to someone else as usual and, of course, they

had had to run away and have a Christian wedding. He was now living in fear of being killed because he had broken the tribal law. He didn't know whether they were following him or if they were just waiting a chance to come for him. So he kept away from us. His name was Daniel.

He was a 'sneaking' sort of person. You never knew when he would pop up beside you. Sometimes we would be taken for picnics and I began to notice that he would never ride in the truck with the others. Yet he would always be there before they were. You wouldn't see him, but after a while you got to know that he would be around some-where. Then as you got out of the truck, up he'd pop right beside you!

One day, I finally managed to talk to him person to person. He really was terror-stricken at the thought of the tribe coming to get him. He told me that the missionary there was the first white man he had ever wanted to live near anyway; he hated all the rest. The missionary had gained Daniel's confidence by helping him to marry his wife, finding employment for them, giving them shelter at first and then later a home. So then I asked him why he hated all other whites so much. He answered me by telling about his mother and the things the white man had done to her.

She used to meet the Adelaide-to-Perth train at Ooldea Station and sell things the local people had made. This could be anything, but it was an important way she and they had of getting a bit more to live on. She used to cry out, 'Two bob! Two bob!' and became quite a well-known character in her way. Whenever a train stopped, there was his mother. This went on for years. Then one day, as the train was pulling to a halt, she went to get on to sell her things, as she always did, when the guard kicked her in the face. She fell from the train and was killed. Daniel had hated all whites after that.

There was yet another time there that will stay in my memory. It was morning and I was on my way to one of our early meetings. I came across a fullblood man bedridden in a camp. The bed he was on was old and dusty, and his

133

mattress and bedding were so filthy that it was going rotten. The poor old fellow was so sick, you see, that he couldn't even get out of bed to relieve himself. You can imagine what it was like. I had to force myself to stop and clean him up, but I knew I had to. The poor old soul.

Anyway I did what I could with his bedding and managed to get him cleaned up. Then I went and found one of the women who, I discovered, was supposed to be looking after him. I took her aside and told her what he should eat and how she should care for him. I already knew she drew rations for him, even though he looked like he hadn't eaten for days. But she wanted more than just the extra rations she got for being in charge of him; she wanted to be paid for looking after him, if she had to do more! Oh, I was very sad about that. I felt so hopeless. What more could we do, I wondered; what were we doing wrong that we weren't really getting through to them?

They had their own policeman on that settlement — a big, bulky man called George. He was always at our meetings, sitting there with great authority. Whether he hindered or helped the attendances, I don't know. All I really remember about George is that when he was called away from a meeting to patch up some difference or other, as he often was, he'd disappear for a while and then return as though nothing had happened. We'd ask him how he got on and he'd always answer very, very wisely, 'I fixed him up!'

Oh, there were other things on the brighter side at Gerard when I think of it. Two of the women once asked me and the other Mission woman if we'd go out fishing with them. We didn't have to bring anything. They had the boat, they said, and the fishing tackle and all that. Well, we jumped at the chance; you don't turn down invitations like that.

But when I climbed into the boat, I couldn't see any bait or lines. Goodness knows how they expected to fish. I didn't say anything, but just sat back and waited. They couldn't be so forgetful as that, surely. Well, we went out in the boat, but still no lines or bait materialised. I was beginning to think that perhaps they had forgotten it, after all. I was dying to say something about it, and I nearly did, but somehow it would have been impolite, so I just kept quiet until they discovered it themselves.

When we got to where we were going to fish, they suddenly produced tiny bits of line, no more than two or three feet long, and gave one to each of us. They had hooks on the ends of them all right, but how, in heaven's name, could anyone catch anything with so short a line? Next, they got out a dish that they used for putting grapes into when they were picking. I noticed it had been greased all around the inside with bits of fat. They then hung another piece of mutton fat over the side of the boat and then tied string to the handles of the dish and dropped it in near the piece of mutton fat. We waited and, after a while, they pulled the dish in. Lo and behold, they had a dishful of yabbies! Big, huge things just hanging on to the fat and caught in the dish. Oh, I had to laugh. But it wasn't over.

What we did then was to use the yabbies as bait on the bits of lines we all had. The water was still very shallow where we were, so we could lower these short lines into the weeds. It wasn't long before we were all catching 'yellow bellies'! My word, I thought, they must be really plentiful down there.

Plentiful they might have been. Yet those women were still amazed that I had caught those fish that day. They told me why. They believed that these fish just didn't bite for anyone; they only took the bait of good women. So that just went to prove that I was a good woman, after all!

We came back to shore eventually and made a fire to cook the fish on. They spread a rug on the ground for us. Now, I might not have told you that they were from Ooldea; they were tribal, with their own language and their own ways. Anyway, they made us understand that it was important that we accept their invitation to sit on that rug if we wanted them to know that we accepted their hospitality. Of course, we gladly did so. They cooked the fish on the coals and made tea in a can they hung over the fire. This was the way they wanted us to know of their thanks and their acceptance of us. The policeman George's wife interpreted for us.

Well, the fish were so burnt, and the tea served in a tin mug didn't look very appetising, either, but we both managed to eat and drink with them. Then I told them that I really would like to see their sort of witchetty grubs. Oh, it was perfectly all right my asking to see them, but, you know, a witchetty grub was about the only thing they never ever brought me!

I asked the head missionary about this later and he said, 'You can get any of them to bring you anything else, but not witchetty grubs. They'll bring you grapes, nuts, fish . . . anything, but not the one thing that is their great delicacy. They won't part with that.'

Goodness, we couldn't eat half of what they brought us. We finally found some willing fowls and fed them on all the grapes they gave us just to use them up!

What we should have done, I suppose, was to give them to all the white ants they had there. They were everywhere. They were so bad that all the buildings had to have concrete floors. I thought that was a bit odd at first, but I soon realised why they had to have them.

Another interesting thing they had at Gerard was a place where unmarried mothers could leave their babies while they went to work. These people were paid for picking and packing the vegetables for market, while the missionaries looked after the babies and young ones. It was an excellent idea. Apart from that, all the people living there were expected to give one hour of each Saturday morning to help improve the mission. The women would sew or anything like that around the place, while the men would do the fencing. They'd even put a telephone line right through to the town and made the road. The Mission was about ten miles from the town, so you could understand why it had taken well over a year to get both of those finished. Oh, and weren't they funny little poles! The trees don't grow very high around there, but they looked almost like dwarfs once they had been stripped down as telephone poles. Anyway, everybody worked that one hour every

Saturday morning — men, women and children. They all did their share. I thought this side of it was a good idea, too.

The people used to make good money while the grapes were on, too. Not only that but they had their own orchard, and grew their own different kinds of nuts. Being so close to the river, you see, they had irrigation, and that was a real blessing.

However, language was a bit of a problem for the four of us. The head missionary thought we wouldn't be able to get through to them because we couldn't speak their language, and I think he was right at first. But they did take notice of us, you know.

Then again, language has always been a real barrier between Aborigines themselves, not just between black and white. For example, later that trip, while we were in Melbourne, we attended a conference of the Institute of Linguistics, which teaches mainly missions. One of my friends from up around the Lismore district was there. He was fluent in the Kumbaingeri language and he was asked to spell words in his language from spoken sounds. He got stuck on one word ... 'white'. There just isn't a Kumbaingeri word for 'white'. At that time I was sitting next to another friend of mine who came from Adelaide and she nudged me to stand up and help him out. She knew we came from the same area basically and thought I'd know the Kumbaingeri equivalent. She thought he just didn't know what the word was. Well, I couldn't help out at all, because I just didn't know Kumbaingeri. I sat there and thought how stupid it was, really. There he was and there I was — two people from around the same sort of area and yet we spoke two entirely different languages. We were only able to communicate with each other in English!

Wherever I've travelled I've found that the case. There are about five hundred different Aboriginal languages. It's not only that, either. Except in isolated parts they have got all mixed up somehow. The true languages — the ones you might think you could learn and then be able

to talk to a whole group of the people from the same area —
are being lost. Despite what a lot say, many of the people
haven't even got their own language to fall back on and
there's no point learning odd words from any of the other
five hundred or so languages.

Well, after we came back from Gerard, we went around
New South Wales quite a lot. There was one part in the
western part of the State I recall particularly. It was called
Gulargambone. It was so sad to compare this place with
Gerard. You couldn't avoid doing so, even if you had wanted
to. The people lived near the Mission, just as they were
doing at Gerard, and they could have had the same thing
there. But there just wasn't the same interest and vitality.
Nobody seemed to care. The Aborigines didn't care; and
the whites didn't care about the Aborigines not caring
about themselves. In fact, I'd say that on the surface
they were even nearer to so-called 'civilisation' than the
people at Gerard. Perhaps that didn't help, despite the
fact that you'd think it should.
    My own husband got terribly involved in the needs of
these Gulargambone people. He went up there with one
of the missionaries, saw the place, and became so depressed
and sorry about the way they were living. He watched the
men coming back from the shearing sheds. They were
earning top money at shearing, yet all they seemed to
want to do with it was to drink until they got so drunk
they'd be absolutely crawling around.
    We lived among these people for a couple of years.
We visited their homes. We tried to help them in any way
they'd let us. We tried our level best to encourage them
to do more with themselves. Oh, my heart used to ache;
I never ever got used to seeing the way they existed. Yet
they didn't take the slightest bit of notice of us, really.
When you tried to speak to them about it, they'd just shrug
and say that nobody cared or wanted them around, so
why bother.
    That was true in a way; there was no denying that.

138

Although they worked hard for him and put plenty of money in his pocket, their white boss was always against them. Yet they were always up early to start work, no matter how bad a night they had had the night before. It just seemed that no matter how much they did or how much they proved themselves, somebody was always 'after' them. Nobody who mattered cared for them.

Oh yes, we went to many places with the UAM — Gilgandra, Wellington, Dubbo. There was always the same need. There were always the fringe dwellers who had to live on the edge of town. They weren't part of the town and they weren't far enough away from the town to be able to, or even have to, look after themselves. The ones that worked in the town could spend their money just like anyone else in the town, oh yes; but they couldn't spend it in a way that would give them dignity, or in any *real* way of spending the fruits of your labour. As I've said, the real cause of it all was this stupid law that said they couldn't go into hotels. Yet nobody hesitated when it came to exploiting them or to actually encouraging them to drink, oh no. Or a taxi would take them near a hotel and the driver would slip in and buy the drink for them. You can imagine how much that was costing them. Oh, they knew how much it was costing them; they weren't stupid. They could see the sheer hypocrisy of it all.

I saw them drinking and drinking and drinking. It used to tear at my heart. There they were working with white men, doing the same job and having to suffer the same things. But they had to wait around like dogs while their workmates went inside. How can you possibly draw the line at who should be treated like a human being and who shouldn't?

But, as I said, those poor people at Gulargambone had it worse than any I've seen. One thing we tried to get going was to get them to build a community hall for themselves.

It didn't have to be a big thing. It only had to be just big enough so that they could meet, talk, play ... a place where the young people could be taught and shown how it was possible to insist on a better way of living for themselves ... that there must be a better way than that which they had been forced into. We even applied to the Aborigines' Welfare Board for some timber for it; we got the people to agree to try at least that. Do you know, the Board rejected the application! It just wasn't interested. Here these people were, willing to build their own community hall if they could get the timber, and now being told no, they couldn't have the timber because it would be better used in building another home.

It wasn't even as if we were asking for something that would cost a fortune. There was plenty of timber lying around. There was plenty at the back of the police station, for example; it'd come from a house that had been pulled down because one of the people had once died in it and now none of them would step inside the door, let alone live in it. So down it came, and the timber was stacked.

So my Joe and I went to see the policeman at the station. It was only to see just how much timber was actually there, but he took us aside and told us that even in the short time that we'd been there he had noticed a marked change in the people there and he wished to goodness that we could stay. But what can you do? The conditions were just too hard in that place. A couple of years would have been enough for anybody there. I know it was for us. It had depressed us so. In the finish my health failed and I had to go down to Sydney for a serious operation. We never returned to Gulargambone; yet I had left my heart behind with those people there. If somebody had only been interested enough!

I took a while to recover, but we still had a lot of places to visit. We went to Kempsey and to Burnt Bridge once a month, and to Forster regularly. Karuah was on our circuit, too. People had suddenly become really interested in the work the Mission had been doing. It was our own churches that were growing with our own pastors and workers. Purfleet had its own Pastor Bert Marr, a saint of a man.

We kept up our interest in La Perouse and Wreck Bay, too, The work that needed to be done never seemed to have an end. Oh, there were many bright spots and many indications that we were getting through to the people. Yet, wherever you turned there were drunks and down-and-outs needing to be lifted out of their hopelessness. Often, particularly in those days, we were the only people they could turn to that they could trust. As soon as they saw us you'd see them doing up their buttons, straightening their trousers or dresses and running their fingers through their hair.

I used to have a good feeling inside me when I saw that they knew somebody cared for them. Something was touching their consciences to do something about their misery.

There were also some amusing times as well. There was when we went down to Melbourne to take part in a festival of nations. Pastor Sir Douglas Nichols, as he is now called, was our host. We had to get up a choir and sing 'Silent Night' in the Aranda tongue. But we had to learn the words first. So, about a week before the festival began, we went along to Doug Nichols' church to rehearse. What really amused me was that it was a white man who had to assist we Aborigines to learn the Aranda words!

Well, eventually we marched through the Melbourne streets. It was a parade showing the different nationalities, all dressed up in their national costumes. It was certainly colourful. Of course, the Australian Aboriginal didn't have a national costume like the others, still one of us got into the act all right. What happened was that the organisers had invited over an African chief, but something went wrong and he wasn't there in time. So they dressed up one of our men, who had come from the western part of New South Wales, and he marched as the African chief. And that's how the Aborigines were represented!

Oh, we had a few laughs over that one. Anyway, we did sing our 'Silent Night' in Aranda and it was very impressive.

It hasn't been at all hard to talk to Aborigines about Christian beliefs. They respond, and I'm positive they do so out of the depths of their hearts. You see, the Aboriginal people have never been idol worshippers. They have always talked about spirits — the spirit of the hills, the spirit in the sun, the spirit in this and the spirit in that. Their spirits weren't dead idols that you could touch; they were in things, living, taking these forms or even human forms. So it was easy to talk to them about the God who was like their greater or higher spirit, and about God the Son and the Holy Spirit; they understood. Many missionaries I've spoken to have said that, too. They aren't fools and their tribal beliefs were not as simple as some say.

You have to keep showing that somebody cares. That somebody is interested. We tried to visit every home and get them interested in things like the culture of their land, their own lost culture, what they could do themselves and what sort of people they could be. All around them they have pressures that make them feel nothing matters. And I can understand how they feel. But by believing in something that is higher and better than ourselves we can overcome these feelings; we can break the drinking habit; we can regain our dignity.

You know, when I think of it, quite a few of us suffered through the years of long hours and hard work. But I believe we left the results of all our joint Mission work in the hearts of the old people . . . and many of the young ones, as well. I often meet people who refer back to the early days of struggle and groping forward to get our message across. They still remember the 'great' things that used to take place, even at Purfleet where we had our own church and pastor. We used to use great big tents with built-up floors because of the crowds who came. Oh yes, it was hard work, but the great interest the people took in our work compensated for that. I even get weary just thinking of all that had to be done just for those meetings alone — kerosene lamps, open fires, carrying your own wood, carting your own water as well as food.

I remember once at Lismore, where we were asked to hold a series of meetings to preach the Gospel, when we had over a hundred people to cater for and it was pouring rain. I even had to get breakfast for them all under these conditions. But we got there; we managed it. We fed them and we prayed with them for a purpose in life, a better way of living, a better way of dressing, better health, better hygiene. And we could see that it made a difference to them.

Times have changed but we proved then what can be done if we all pull together and work hard and unselfishly to help each other to get back the dignity and standard of living we have lost. In the old days our people lived in harmony with their own laws and culture. Those laws were strict but just. The culture gave a meaning and purpose to life. The people didn't have the feeling of hopelessness I have seen so much of in my day. The Aboriginal has to identify himself with this and be proud of it as I have learned to be. Then, he has to go on to be a part of this changing world; not to be beaten by it; to take the best of both cultures, not the worst. We still need to believe in a higher power, a great spirit outside ourselves; to me, this power is called God, or the Holy Spirit.

14

THE DEAR LITTLE
THING KNEW

The Gillawarra Gift Shop helped many people in my ten years. There was one particular scheme, started by a local school teacher, in which we sent some of the kiddies away each year to stay with families in Newcastle. The Rotary Club of Newcastle supported and organised it.

We would send fourteen children at a time. We felt that it was good for them to live in other people's homes and see how they lived. It was more than that, too. They not only saw how they lived, but had to come up against that different life style and learn to live alongside of it. I suppose you could say it was working at assimilation in a practical way. It was a lot of hard work for those of us on the shop committee to get the right children to go to the right home, but on the whole it was worth it.

For many of the kiddies it was their very first trip away from home. I used to go with them and visit each family just to make sure they were going to be all right, while I was waiting for the train to bring me back. That wasn't the hardest part by a long shot. The most difficult thing was getting them organised from our end. We made sure that the children had the right clothes and that those right clothes were good clothes. Whenever somebody in the town gave us fairly good clothes, I'd put them aside for the kiddies going to stay in Newcastle. I just felt that they had to go with their heads up high, otherwise there was no point in the scheme at all.

Just before they were due to leave we'd ask them all to bring their little bags along so that we could see just what they didn't have. Then we'd set to and start sewing and mending like mad. The St Vincent de Paul people were marvellous in this respect. Eventually the day that they were to leave would come around.

The kids would stand on the verandah of the shop, all brushed up neat and tidy, all with great big grins on their faces. There'd always be a last one who would be running late, so some of them would rush off to see what was the matter. Then they'd come back pleased as punch because their friend wasn't going to be left behind, but was hurrying as fast as he or she could. Oh, it was lovely just to watch their faces.

I had a machine in the shop and I used to sit down and sew sometimes until one or two o'clock in the morning to ensure they all had decent things to wear. Then, if they didn't have a toothbrush or somesuch, I'd ring Max Carey, the chemist on the shop committee, and mention that this or that was needed, and sure enough he'd drive out with it.

We had our little disappointments, but they were to be expected. Some of the kiddies wouldn't behave, but not as many of them as you had a right to expect. I even found that that scheme was good for their mothers as well. They could have a few weeks' break from their children for just that little breather, and they did so appreciate it even if they wouldn't admit they did.

You know, some of our kiddies couldn't even use a knife or fork at the time they went away. That soon changed when they moved in with a family in Newcastle, though. Many of the families would ask to have the same child back to stay next year. They would look forward to seeing the child, as much as the child was looking forward to going back. Then again, some of them would stay right over the whole holidays. Of course, they took a few days to get settled in. That was only natural, because they lived in such small groups at Purfleet that the thought of being on their own for any time frightened a lot of them. Occasionally we would get a phone call saying so-and-so wanted to come home and we'd talk to the child. Some of them just wanted to hear our voices, I think, but some of them were genuinely unhappy and, in that case, we usually got them somewhere else to stay, preferably with one of the other kiddies.

Education comes to mind now. People are always talking about education this and education that. Teachers ringing up because kiddies are away from school, and all that. As I said before, these same children have parents who went to school for years without being taught anything. They came out of school after all those years scarcely able to read.

I saw it happen in my own family. They all went to school at Purfleet for about ten years and could scarcely spell their own names! No wonder the older people weren't interested in their children going to school. What did it matter if the kid missed a day or two here and there? What had education to do with attending school? Whether you had education or not, you still lived the same; you still just got by like everyone else.

Well, that was another thing about the Gillawarra Gift Shop ... the children we were able to help. The first I remember was the daughter of a cousin of mine. She lived at Forster, and she was a very bright girl. That was obvious. The father had died. Anyway, at that time we used to visit Forster and have a weekly women's meeting. One day this cousin came up to me with the girl and said she wanted to come down to Taree High School. She wanted to go on with school and Forster didn't have a high school at that stage.

I had always wanted to prove that an Aboriginal child could be educated just as well as any other, so I decided to see what I could do about it. I got on to a person I knew who lived in Taree, Mr Brown, and he said he would gladly take an interest in young Bev, as her name is. He opened

146

up his house to her, so that she wouldn't have to make the long and lonely bus trip in and out each day. He had a daughter the same age as Bev and they became firm friends. She was helped with books and clothes and everything she might need. Everybody was good to her.

Yet the girl was still lonely. She probably felt guilty about leaving her mother in Forster to cope with the four other children on her own. Not even staying with a girl of her own age, and going to parties and things, made her less homesick. So the next thing I tried was to go back to Forster and see her mother. I asked her if she would be willing to come down to Purfleet to live, if I could get a home for her. It took a lot to convince her, but finally she said all right; like so many of the people, she wanted her kids to have what she never had.

So I came back to Purfleet and got on to the Manager. He said he would see what he could do about getting them somewhere to live there. As it happened a house came up soon after that, so we went along and cleaned it up for her. We even got in food for the family and wood for the fire. By this time the people had got interested in helping this little girl get a proper education, and came along and helped, too.

Anyway, to cut a long story short, we got her family settled in, and from there Bev started on her hard task. She was going to Tech to learn shorthand and typing and was going pretty good, too. One night I went over to see how she was getting on. I found her sitting in an almost dark room trying to read her books. All she had was an old fat light — an old home-made one with a wick of rag coiled around in a tin with fat in it. There they were ... it sparkling and spluttering and poor little Bev hovering over her books trying to read by it!

Well, she had to have something so that she could at least *see* her books. So we got up an appeal and got her a proper lamp. It wasn't much of a problem, I know, but it does demonstrate what the people had to go through, doesn't it?

There was a good kid! She stuck to her guns. She knew

that one day she would win through and, sure enough, that day came. She passed all her exams with flying colours. Oh, I was so proud of her! Then the Board got her a job in Sydney with the government stores — the place that among other things used to fill out all the orders for food and clothing for the Aboriginal people. She became the first Aboriginal to work there and the first who was able to use an electric typewriter. How's that for someone who didn't have electricity on at home!

I remember she used to have to teach people who came in to buy typewriters how to type . . . especially the police. They were changing over to the new electric type then and I remember one of her letters back to her Mum saying, 'Mum, I am sitting here with a big cop standing over my shoulder. I feel so frightened.'

She wouldn't have been joking. There has always been this latent fear of the police in Aborigines — with good reason, too. It's because the police hardly ever come to an Aboriginal with good news. It's always bad news, probably arresting the husband and father for just being drunk, and things like that. So there was this poor little girl with this kind of fear in her heart and a natural loneliness for home. But she stuck it out, and she made it. She's with the Housing Commission now and married with three children. A modern working mum in the great big city of Sydney!

The second one we were able to help was Ray. His family was having a rough time of it — rougher even than was normal. They didn't have a home of their own but had to share one with somebody else. Ray's father had told me that he had so many children — and he did — that he couldn't afford to keep the boy in school any longer. He said that the boy just had to go out and get a job and help out. But I knew the boy badly wanted to go on with his schooling, so we got the shop committee together again to see what could be done. We decided we'd have a go at helping Ray get through school.

It was arranged that he would come and live at my place for his last year of study, which he did. He passed his exams with no trouble at all. But that wasn't the end of it.

He applied for the Air Force and got in easily. He trained as a mechanic and was working on the new jet planes. He did very well and he was told he was a good mechanic. He married and had two children. He was even sent to Malaysia and they spent two or three years there. Then the time came for him to come back to Australia again. He was still being told how good his work was and he was given a lot of responsibility, a lot of really difficult jobs. I was so proud of him. He felt let down in his own way, though. There was no promotion for Ray. Other lads were getting promotions and I know he wondered where he went wrong. He got such good reports, but no promotion.

He wanted to come back home when he'd finished his time. They both missed their families and he loved the river and the coast. The kids had started school, too. He knew he still wouldn't get a job, but he wanted to go into the fishing business with his father.

I often think about some of those I tried to help. When any of them asked me where did they go wrong, why didn't they get anywhere after all their work, I didn't know what to say. What could I tell them? I know some of these kids are going to really make it—some of them are starting to now. They'll be good at sport, good at jobs, good at anything they try—if they are only given a chance. That was the only sort of thing I could tell them. Ray's still working hard at making a life for himself and his family, so all that effort was worth it.

There was another boy, Paul. He got into Tech. We hoped he was going to be a really good artist one day because his father was a good artist in the traditional Aboriginal way. One of my boys was good at art, too, and Paul copied them. So we decided to help Paul. We bought him some paints and a few clothes and off he went.

But he didn't last long at Tech. His father got a job and a house in Newcastle when the system changed, and the family moved down there. I wanted Paul to stay, but he naturally wanted to follow the family.

There were quite a few we tried to get interested in doing more with their lives by going to Tech. It was a long way from where we were, though, and they always had the problem of getting in and out at night. I felt at times that I was the only one pushing them to go. If I tried too hard to push them, it looked as if I was interfering, so in the finish I didn't know what to do. I hadn't been allowed to get far with my education; then I'd wanted so badly to train as a nurse and we weren't allowed. Now that we were at last able to get a decent education and do the extra training, I was in a hurry for those kids to make the most of it. But it's hard to undo all the years of being told you're not good enough to be educated properly or to get a decent job. It's going to take a long time to break that pattern.

There were other ways we helped the kids through that shop. We didn't have any medical service then, so I used to take some of them down to the city for treatment. It was a long trip then. You sat up all night or all day to get there by train. There was one little girl I particularly remember, Polly Ann. She was a dear little thing. She was a spastic kiddy. She spent a lot of time in hospital; she couldn't walk, she couldn't talk. It was so sad. Since I've been able to watch television, I've seen so many sad cases that remind me of that girl. What can you do?

The trouble was, there was really nobody who could help her except in the city, which was a long way away and expensive. We decided to try to help her and I offered to take her to Sydney for tests and treatment. The family couldn't afford to take her and they had other children to worry about as well.

Taking her to Sydney on that train wasn't easy. She could sit up but she couldn't feed herself or do anything. She was a big kiddy, too, and she could be very difficult at times. There were many sympathetic people who helped, though. You don't realise how kind people can be, complete strangers some of them, until you have a real problem like that. At the other end, we'd have to wait at the station, at the Travellers' Aid, because we were too early to go anywhere. They were very good. They let me wash and change her there as she had to be treated like a baby. Some of those trips were there and back in one day, but sometimes I'd have to stay for a week while she was having tests or special treatment. Then I would have to go all the way out to a hostel in La Perouse, the only place where I could stay. Some of the church people from there would take me into the hospital or out to the Spastic Centre each day. Even the Board helped with the accommodation and let me keep her there as well.

Then I would bring Polly Ann all the way home again. We'd arrive very early in the morning and I'd let her sleep at my place until it was light. I don't think anyone realised what I went through just for that one child, but what else could you do? You have to try to help. They said in Sydney that the tests showed there wasn't much hope for her to improve. They made her special boots to try to help her to walk, but she needed hours spent on her each day just to look after her. It was too much for the family without any specialist help. They couldn't handle her. It was a full-time job each day and she didn't improve at all.

The case got so sad that I finally went to the Manager and told him he should do something. He said the best thing was to try to get her into a home. This is always a problem in the country because it means they have to be taken to the city. Anyway, he saw the mother and she agreed because she had a couple of babies and she couldn't manage her. The Manager was to take her to Newcastle and they asked me if I would go because Polly Ann was so fond of me. The poor little pet was so pleased to see me again that I went along. I will never forget that trip. When we got to Wootton, the Manager wanted to call in to see a friend of his. He left us sitting in the car. Polly Ann had her dolly with her. She knew how to dress her dolly and she was playing with it. Then suddenly she began to cry. She must have started to think of home. The tears just rolled down her cheeks and she clung hard to that old doll. I thought then that despite what everyone said about her not having much intelligence, despite all those tests she'd been given to prove it, the poor little thing knew she was being taken away and wouldn't be going home again.

When we got to the home, they examined her thoroughly. They were very kind to her. One of the young fellows took her by the hand and tried to make her walk. She couldn't. Oh, it was so sad leaving her, but we had to get back.

I didn't see her again. I asked a few people down there to look in when they could. One of them told me that she did learn to walk, but still couldn't talk. Finally I heard that she had ended up in a psychiatric hospital. They had given her up as hopeless.

I often think of that trip down to Newcastle. I can sympathise with people having to make the same decision. I've helped a few people since then, just by being a sympathetic listener; that's often as much as anyone can do, but there's not many who do it. But then, not many have been through what we went through with Polly Ann.

The shop used to help the mothers, too. We had the policy that, if we could, we would lend them money if they hadn't any left from their pensions. The idea was that they should learn to save and manage their own affairs. That was what the shop was really there for . . . to teach the people how to manage their own money affairs.

The condition of the loans was that they must pay the money back to the shop no matter how long it took them. Some of them would be a little bit forgetful and I'd have to go to them and explain to them that the shop wouldn't have any money if everybody forgot to repay their loan, and if there was no money there wouldn't be any loans to others. They soon started to get the idea that we were all helping each other, and they would come.

152

I remember one woman in particular. Her husband was working on the railway for a long time and got hurt in some accident or other. He had to go into hospital in Quirindi. She was distressed. She couldn't afford to go out there to visit him and she couldn't get any compensation money through because of all the red tape at the time. So finally we loaned her the money for petrol so that she could drive out to visit him. When she got there she asked for permission to have him moved down to Taree Hospital, but they told her she'd have to pay for the ambulance if she wanted to do that. Well, that wasn't on, so she just brought him back in the back of their old station wagon!

By then, of course, they had no food. They had three small children. So we got in touch with the St Vincent de Paul people who managed to get them rations for a few weeks at least. They said they couldn't give any more because it might further complicate the compensation mix-up. Well, the shop stepped in and gave them their orders of food. It was really straining our resources to the limit at that time. But we did it, and we managed to get our money back, too.

To this day her husband has spoken up for the Gillawarra Gift Shop, even after the 'Black Power' people and the other critics had come in and started to condemn us for not ever doing anything for the people ... just spent the money on ourselves. He still stands up and says that if it wasn't for us being in the shop his children would have starved to death. That sort of thing makes you know that you did something a little worthwhile anyway.

Oh, there were several cases where the husband had been put in gaol and his family left without any food. I would allow them to have so much money for buying what they needed or I would get on to any organisation that might help them out if we had no spare cash at the time. But what made such situations as that worse was that the husband would be thrown into gaol just for being drunk. They'd get a month or more just for being that. In the meantime their families just had to starve and that

153

was what was criminal, not the man being drunk. It wasn't as though it was unusual, either. That sort of thing used to go on a lot. Fortunately times have changed, and not before time. Even if they are hauled up for being drunk nowadays, it's only rarely that they throw them in gaol. They might as well have thrown the whole family in, too, back in those days.

The shop didn't only have women sitting around sipping cups of tea, oh no. We had tourist buses calling in all the time, and they'd stop for a couple of hours sometimes. The Manager would come over and help with the money while I was being run off my feet. They even used to have me standing on the verandah giving the tourists a talk about Purfleet and about the Aboriginal people in general. The questions they kept asking me! I'd get a bit on edge — you know, trying to run around and do everything but having to stop and answer the same old questions again and again.

But I always made myself stop and answer as best I could. I wanted those tourists to leave with just a little bit more knowledge about the Aborigines than when they arrived. I wanted to try to get through to them what exactly being an Aboriginal meant, and exactly what being an Aboriginal felt like.

15

A RIGHT OLD
CON MAN

One day a man called at the shop and started to talk to me about marching girls. That was odd enough in itself, because I had hardly ever heard of such a thing let alone talking about it in the Gillawarra shop.

Then he came out with what he was really there for. He said he wanted to do something for the children of Purfleet and what did I think about him forming the Purfleet Marching Girls Team? The first thing that popped into my mouth was, 'I wouldn't want our girls to be exploited', but he swore he wouldn't do that.

Anyway we called the people together and asked them what they thought about the idea. Most of them were in favour of it. In fact the whole settlement really became excited about the prospect. So we formed a committee and we set about getting it organised. One of the first things to do was prepare a suitable area where the girls could train. The Manager was still resident then and he allowed his men to come over and help level off a piece of land right alongside the shop. We even rigged up an outside light so that they could train at night.

What made the whole thing seem even better was that this man proved a very good trainer. He had a team — and a good one at that — in shape in no time.

155

Then we set about getting the uniforms. They looked good on the girls, too. The girls threw themselves into training and becoming a top team. It wasn't long before they were travelling everywhere — even to Melbourne and Brisbane. They did really well in the competitions, too; got a lot of publicity and made us very proud of them.

The only worrying thing about the whole affair was that this man always seemed to be after money. He always seemed short of it, even after he'd got the many donations that used to come his way. We started to get the feeling that things were not all they seemed to be.

It was about this time that he started a raffle without us even knowing it. I don't know, it was some way he was doing the books. You could suspect, but you couldn't ever actually catch him out on anything. Besides, the girls were loving it, so there didn't seem to be any grounds for our nagging suspicions.

One day the police came to see me. They asked me if I knew anything about this man at all. I told them I didn't know much about him at all really. All I knew was that he seemed to be doing a marvellous job with the team. They went away.

Then, soon after that incident, a police sergeant came to the shop and asked me if I knew anything about a raffle for the Purfleet Marching Girls. I knew absolutely nothing about that, not a thing. It appeared that this man had been staying at a motel just a little way away and somehow or other they had found a swag of raffle butts in his room. Then someone from the local RSL had informed them he'd been through the club selling tickets! Oh, he turned out a right old con man, he did.

The poor kids, they were so disappointed. You had to feel sorry for them. But it wasn't only that time in the RSL that this man had used their name. Apparently he would stand near a hotel — Coopernook Hotel was one he did this in front of — laid a blanket on the ground, and got the children to march past there. People would throw money on to the blanket in appreciation! Oh, the children had begun to hint that something like this was going on, but it was a bit hard to believe and, anyway, when I'd have a go at him about it, he would hotly deny it all the time.

Well, he shot through with the police on his tail. We never heard what became of him. There was a rumour that he went away to Western Australia somewhere, but who knows whether he did or not. The silly thing was he was a splendid teacher. He knew his business all right and, what was rarer, he knew how to get the best out of the kiddies without dampening their enthusiasm.

After he had gone one of the older girls tried to lead them, but there wasn't the same enthusiasm any more. They soon lost interest in the marching girls movement. That was a great pity, you know, after all those months of hard work they had put in. I will never forget the day they marched along Taree's main street. I was so proud of them and they looked so lovely. They were clapped and cheered ... and then for that man to do such a thing as that to them! Somehow the people seemed to get let down all the time.

16

THIS WAS MY JOE

My husband, Joe, was ill for many years. Towards the end of his life we used to go down to the beach after I had finished work. He had always felt at one with the sea, and I hoped the trip would tire him out enough so he could sleep at night. But it rarely did.

He'd have whole nights of walking around and sitting, just being totally unable to rest at all. Oh, only God knows the sufferings of human beings. The doctor finally had to admit that he couldn't do anything more and put him in hospital. He only went along when I promised that I'd visit him there every day. He knew he would be so lonely.

One day I knew I couldn't get to the hospital until well after dark, so I asked my nephew if he would drive me there. His wife and another friend of theirs came along as well. We no sooner got on to the highway when the car's lights failed. It was a fuse, and it was such a pitch black night outside. Anyway, we stopped and my nephew asked his wife to look around for a piece of chocolate silver paper or something that might be lying about on the side of the road that he could use for a fuse. She got out and that was the last thing I remember for a while.

She told me — later, of course — that she was just about

to pick up a piece when she suddenly saw the car rearing up into the air! What happened was a car coming the other way crashed into us and then one coming from behind us did the same.

The first crash caused me to hit my head and then the second one threw me forward so that I cracked two of my ribs. Well, I know I easily could have been killed, but I only mention this to tell you how I ended up in the same hospital as my Joe! I had concussion and those broken ribs. Thank goodness the others were luckier and only got a bit shaken up because they thought I was really very hurt.

Anyway, at the hospital, I finally managed to ask the doctor whether he would tell Joe why I hadn't come on time and that I wasn't too bad. He did. Not only that, but he was kind enough to have me taken up to Joe when I was well enough, so that he could see for himself that I was all right. After a couple of days I was allowed home. At least at home I could keep busy to force my mind away from things, but, try as hard as I could I still felt the emptiness of the house without the one I so dearly loved. We had been together for so long ... thirty-three years ... he was almost a part of me. And there he was, not near me anymore; his dear life slipping away and I couldn't do a thing about it. I just refused to think of the possibility that I might have to give him up. My Joe.

Oh, he was a peaceful, loving man. He was big. He was strong. He was proud. And he had so many good friends, even some businessmen in town with whom he used to go fishing. Not once in his whole life did he stop loving his children, not for one single moment, even though they caused him many a heartache. As for him and me? All I can say is that it seemed a horrible eternity to have to watch my poor Joe slowly deteriorate, right from years before he finished up in hospital.

His steps had been getting slower, his body thinner. Each day, each year, I watched this. Finally we no longer went out in the car and we no longer sang together. I'd be fearful at night because of his shortness of breath and that pain in his chest. Yet all the love I had in the world to give him couldn't ease it for him. No matter how tired he was we wouldn't be in bed long before he'd have to get up again and sit by the fire hoping he might find some way to relieve the pain. My heart was sick and my faith in God strained to the limit. But I held on with all the force I could muster to will my Joe better.

As I said, the doctor gave up and put him into hospital. Drugs no longer did anything, and yet both of us kept hoping that something miraculous would happen. It didn't, if you don't count the wonderful years we had together.

You know, I still love my Joe as much as I did the day we first met. Someday we will meet again and there won't be any pain and there won't be any need to ache with all your being for a miracle. I believe that passionately.

Joe always wore a hat pulled down over his forehead when he went anywhere. He would never look at anyone unless they spoke first. This wasn't because he disliked people. He'd given so much of his life over to helping too many people to dislike them. It was just the way he had been brought up and probably because of the sadness he must have gone through with his mother leaving him so early in his life. I think that had a lot to do with the way he was.

My Joe was a true Aboriginal man. He scarcely spoke to anyone. He was always proper in his behaviour, fond of laughter and jokes. He could amuse the kiddies like nobody could because he was skilful with his hands. This made him a good mimicker and the children loved it. Yes, he was big, but not even in the roughest game of football that you would ever come across did I ever see him lose his temper. That applied when it came to his children, too. He was lively and good company with his family, yet so quiet with other people that it used to make you wonder sometimes. Even under all sorts of privations in our home he would show, yes, a great delicacy of feeling. What's more, he was honest to the hilt, too; he never took any single person down for anything. He wouldn't lie even to save my life, as I used to tell him.

Do you know, he never called me by my name. That's true. If he had to call me anything, it was always 'wife'. One time, when we were living out west, I asked him if he'd just say my name sometimes because, being away from home, I hardly ever had the chance to hear it! He nodded and understood, but he never got around to it. It was his way.

I had a very dear friend who was married to one of my uncles, and she never left my side during all this time of Joe's pain and suffering. I'd be up at the hospital by his side with those screens that they put around the bed when somebody's really ill . . . and in the early hours of the morning one of the screens would be drawn quietly apart and there she'd be, by my side for the rest of the night.

Joe was restless at this stage; he'd had so many drugs for the pain that he had started to crave for them. How cursed was this stuff that he'd been given for his heart! He'd just lie there and say over and over again, 'Go and get me a tablet'. And I couldn't do anything for him. My heart would be frozen. I knew I couldn't get him a tablet.

The end came. The doctor called me in to say that Joe wasn't responding and there was nothing else that could be done. But for days and nights he fought for his life. He was a fighter. This was my Joe.

I'd been up all night with him and I had just returned home to have breakfast and to have a shower before going back there, when the phone message came to say he'd passed on. Oh, and I wasn't even there when he left me. We laid him to rest in the old Aboriginal cemetery where most of the ones from so long ago are buried.

I had three grandchildren with me. They were company at night after I had finished for the day at the shop. Two of them were still going to school and at least they kept me busy for a while. I tried to keep on the go as much as I could. It kept my mind from wandering back to my Joe.

Then, one day not soon after that, I got notice to quit my home. It had been condemned. On top of everything, this really shook me up. When you've been in a place for so long ... you've settled there ... you've created your memories in it and put down roots ... you belong there, and that's all there is to it. Then, to be told you have to move, just like that ... !

This was another change, another 'improvement'. But, like the Manager's arrival, I was told by government authorities to get out of my home. The Housing Commission took over the houses and condemned mine because it was not up to their standards. It was the old school house, but we'd had it renovated — put a bathroom in, had the electricity put on, and all at our own expense. It was better than some of the others, but not in the Commission's eyes.

I hadn't the slightest idea where I was going. There were no empty houses at Purfleet. I had to fill in those forms for the Housing Commission to get a house, but I had no idea where it might be, and I just had to wait. Every so often the new authorities would ring me at the shop, 'When will you be moving out?', 'How long before you'll be leaving?' etc. etc. Then I'd start to worry about it all over again. There wasn't a thing I could do no matter how much I worried about it; I just had to wait. You know, I think one of the greatest things a person can learn in life is how to wait for things. Well, here I was, an impatient person, always wanting things over and done with. I *hated* waiting.

Finally I moved. It was on St Patrick's Day. I was going back to live town side, right near where I was born ... from where I had been carried as a tiny child out to the Purfleet reserve. I felt I had come full circle.

I got away from Purfleet early in the morning. I didn't want anybody to peek out from behind their curtains when I was coming, and I wanted to leave the reserve before everyone was up. It was better that way. I would have been too upset and I couldn't take any more. I'd ordered the lorry to go and pick up the rest of my stuff that I hadn't shifted in the night or in the afternoons, bit by bit.

I was terrified of having to move back to the town. I knew what people would say. I still didn't belong with either black or white.

Well, the house turned out to be a bit bigger than what I was used to and, in the next few days, two dear friends of mine came in to help me. They put a nail here, a nail there, put the curtains up and so forth ... all the sorts of jobs my dear Joe would have done. I suddenly missed him so horribly again. I longed to tell him things or show him this or that. I'd have to stop myself from actually starting to do so. It was a time, too, when I think back on it now, that I seemed to lose my memories, both the beautiful and the sad. They somehow left me. There I was having to cope with having to be uprooted, alone, and having a strong sense that my memories were being smashed all to pieces as they pulled down my old home and ruined my beautiful garden.

It didn't help to hear, either ... and this was just as soon after I moved in as I had expected ... the same old hurtful remark, 'I wonder why this old black woman got a house when so many whites need homes?' If only they knew how much I'd wanted to stay in my old home!

After all this, all I could do was work at the shop, look after my grandchildren and try my hardest to go on. Even that came unstuck. I was having a shower one morning and noticed something that really rocked me. It was a lump in my breast. And it proved to be what I feared.

The day came for the operation and I was back again in a hospital bed. It was the same year, incidentally, that I had been named 'Lady of the Year' by Quota. I'll never forget how those ladies from the CWA visited me in turns and brought me such lovely flowers. I never wanted for anything. I can tell you this, too: I never cried so much

163

as I did one day when I was lying there feeling so alone, when all of a sudden so many of my friends were there loading me down with a whole lot of beautiful flowers. The tears that I'd built up for so long all burst out at once.

17

ABORIGINAL BLOOD
CAN'T

I have come up against discrimination all my life. I can
tell you that discrimination isn't all from the one side,
either. I got it from the Aboriginal side, too.

I don't know ... the whites thought the Aborigines
'stupid' and the Aborigines thought the same thing about
the whites. Personally, it came at me from both sides.

It used to be most noticeable and the most hateful
at the picture show. The black people used to have to sit
down at the very front, looking straight up at the screen.
They weren't allowed to sit anywhere else. They used
to be marched down there when the lights were dim,
because the managements were ashamed to let their white
customers see just how many black people they were letting
in. If they could have completely stopped all Aboriginal
people from going to the pictures at all, I believe they would
have, you know. This sort of thing wasn't too long ago,
either.

I had one unforgettable experience that I never want
to go through again. It was up at Forster. I used to work
there each year during the holidays. Joe would take the
tourists out fishing and I would work in a guest house.
I used to get to know some guests pretty well, year in
and year out. Anyway, this year some of them bought me

a couple of the best tickets in the house for a certain picture.

Now, I had heard about this discrimination and I thought Joe and I would go along anyway to see if it really was true. I couldn't really believe it at the time, you see. Well, we walked into that picture house, down the aisle, found our row and sat in our reserved seats. The next thing we knew was the usher telling us we'd have to move because we weren't allowed to sit there! I replied that we had the reserved seats and we intended to sit where we'd paid for.

Oh, he wouldn't hear of this. They had a roped off row right down the front for us Aborigines and that's where we had to sit. I wouldn't hear of that, either. I didn't care what fuss I made. I refused to move and demanded to see the manager. But he wouldn't come out and see me, oh no; I had to go out to his office. So I did, and I asked him for an explanation. You know, he told us the same thing; the roped off area was for us.

Well, that was just too much. I told him what I thought of him. He tried to wriggle out of it by saying that he didn't want to lose his other customers, but it was just all so weak. Joe and I left that place and I have never been back. We had proved that discrimination existed, all right.

In the early days the people of Purfleet would walk the two miles backwards and forwards to see the picture shows when the first picture theatre opened in Taree. It was owned by the Ikens. An Aboriginal woman used to work for Mrs Ikens, so she used to let the people sit where they wanted to. Not that it was anything palatial in those days, mind you. There was just an earth floor and hard seats for everybody, white or black. The whole place was just a big tin place with lots of fig trees growing around it. You'd be sitting there and all of a sudden there would be a possum running up and down along the top of the tin, and its shadow would be flitting all over the screen. It used to be a laugh.

166

I even came up against discrimination in homes that I was actually working in, if you can believe that. Some of those people would make me have my meals outside on a special old plate, and sterilise my knife and fork afterwards! Again, that was in the bad old days. Yet I've also worked in hotels where the Aboriginal wasn't even allowed to go by law. We were allowed to work there doing the dirty jobs all right!

It's my opinion that middle-class white people were more prejudiced than any. I think it was because of their ignorance. They just didn't know what the Aboriginal person was like at all. When they heard that the people were diseased, didn't wash and weren't clean, that was good enough for them. They wouldn't bother to find out the real situation, let alone doubt it. They wouldn't have to look too long to see that the Aborigines love to swim, especially the children and the young folk. They'd swim all day if given the chance. But, what's the good of that, if you haven't good clothes to change back into? My grandmother was very strict about cleanliness and hygiene — that stick of hers helped to remind us. There are a lot of families like ours. Some aren't but that's not because they're Aboriginal — they're just lazy!

It's in that area that I get so mad. I hate that sort of ignorance. The whites could have been so sympathetic without much cost to themselves. They could have helped the children at least. They could have put the energy into teaching the kiddies. But no. Instead, when they saw you in the street, they would scarcely speak to you in passing in case somebody saw that they knew an 'Abo'. And, frankly, that sort of thing just stank.

Let me tell you about the rights we were supposed to have in theory, too. When I was working for the bank manager in Sydney I came of age. One day he asked me whether I was on the electoral roll. I told him I wasn't. He said I ought to be, so I went along and had my name put on the roll there.

The next elections came along and I went along with the family to vote with them. That felt good. I was pleased about that, being able to cast my vote and feeling that I had a belonging somewhere. It doesn't matter if I can't remember who I voted for; I felt I had really become an adult.

Anyway I was back here when the next election after that came along. On voting day I rolled up at the polling booth at Glenthorne and told them that I was on the roll in Sydney but not at Taree. 'Oh,' the man said, 'you're not eligible to vote. People with Aboriginal blood aren't allowed to vote. That's the law.'

I stood there amazed and asked him would he kindly repeat that. 'I just told you,' he said. 'You're not allowed to vote.' Just then I saw some people I knew come in and cast their votes. Nobody tried to stop them. Oh, they had Aboriginal 'blood' all right, but their skins were much lighter. I watched them put their papers in the ballot box, and then turned to this white person and asked him if he would kindly tell me why there was one law for some people and another for others. He didn't like that at all, but by now I had made him really uncomfortable, you see. I know why that was. He was having to *think* about what he had told me. Anyway, I knew I wouldn't get any further that day, so I left it at that.

Well, the next time to vote came around and I got word that this man — I had actually worked for him once — had had my name put on the roll there! So once more I went down to the polling booth on the proper day and, sure enough, there were a couple of those other Aborigines putting their vote forward. They were working and living on the farms thereabouts, so they were on the roll. As it turned out, do you know the real reason why they had had the hide to stop me from voting? The real reason was simply because I lived at Purfleet! Because we lived in the 'Black's Camp' we couldn't vote, and that's the truth. And that's one reason I said that I think the middle-class whites are the worst when it comes to prejudice. They don't *think* about what they're doing. It was enough just to dismiss all the people living out in the 'Black's Camp', because if you lived out there you just had to be no-hopers, you see.

Can you wonder why things were as they were with the people on reserves? What hope did we have? From the day you were born all you ever heard about was how you came from the 'Black's Camp'. You weren't a person; you were just a thing who had to live out there to keep you away from decent people. It is not too different even today, either. It really doesn't matter if they've got lovely homes out there now, kept nicely as anyone's and with all mod cons. No, you still come from the 'Black's Camp'. It's never the Purfleet 'area' or the Purfleet 'village' or 'town'. I've even heard church people calling it the 'Black's Camp' and they were the people I expected would do the most to break down such prejudice. And that was particularly hurtful to me, especially since I have always believed in the church so.

The people at Purfleet finally managed to get on the electoral roll when the Manager-system started there. One of the Manager's jobs was to make sure those eligible people knew they were eligible and had the right to vote. But, you know, some of the people were still very reluctant to go on the roll. I really don't think they understood what was going on, and that it scared them a bit. That's why, when I was in the shop, I felt so strongly that I should try to do as much as I could to make them understand what voting really meant.

I had a terrible job trying to get the people to understand that they not only had to be on the roll, but they *should* be on the roll. They were a part of this country, and a part of making this country even better. Finally the older ones, as afraid as they still were, put their names down. Let me try to explain why they were 'afraid'. It wasn't that they were uneducated, or couldn't understand, or found it hard to change their ways when it came to dealing with the white world. No, it wasn't those things. You see,

169

if voting is compulsory — you have to do it, you have to vote as they kept being told — that made it for them part of the *law*; and in their eyes, the *law* meant policemen and arrest and bad news and being roughed around. It was the same kind of fear that had been in the hearts of these people for so very long, right from the earliest of days. In fact, it went right back to the days when they used to come and try to take their children away because the *law* said the children had to go. The women would be crying and the children hiding in the bush — those were the kinds of feeling that words like 'compulsory' and 'law' aroused in them, even sometimes the younger ones. You have to understand that to understand why they were so reluctant. It wasn't just ignorance at all.

Well, things have changed now, and they're mostly all on the roll. We got a lot of help from the people on the shop committee in getting this sorted out. But while I can say that things have changed, I have to say that change has brought a lot of heartache with it, too ... a lot of problems of adjustment to something new when you had just thought you had adjusted to something new. Everything is shifting all the time.

One time — it was so funny — I was helping-out for the Country Party in the street by the shop. There was a man across the way from me doing the same thing, but for the Labor Party. Anyway, I'd always make a cup of tea and take along something to eat for the people being officials there. This day was a terribly hot one, so I invited the Labor man over to have a cuppa with us. He was so intrigued that we should ask him! He said that it was the very first polling booth he had been at where he had been given a cup of tea — and this was by the opposition! So he had his cuppa and some sandwiches and then went back to his post.

Not long afterwards I received a box of handkerchiefs through the post. It was from that Labor man. He asked me to accept this little gift from him with his thanks for giving him a drink that boiling day, just when he couldn't see where he was even going to get a drink of water!

As for that discrimination at the pictures ... that was finally broken down, and not before time. Incidentally, the person who finally gave the order for no discrimination was the very same man who had asked me to leave the theatre that time in Forster. How that came about was this: as I said, I was the first president of the Purfleet Branch of the CWA. As such I was a delegate to a CWA convention. Well, I got to talking with this woman and then found out she was the wife of the same picture theatre manager! Anyway, soon after that there was a sort of get-together in Taree and she asked her husband to pick me up and give me a lift.

It was the first time that I had met him after that incident. I don't know whether she did it deliberately or not, but she left us alone in the car for a while and we had a really good talk.

He hadn't forgotten me. He said he never would! He told me that afterwards he had given instructions that Aboriginal people could sit where they liked and hang the regular customers. The odd thing was, he said, that they still seemed afraid that someone would say something and sat down the front anyway. Some of them still waited for the lights to go out before they went to their seats, in case something nasty was said to them. They had got so used to being treated like that that they couldn't get out of the habit!

There was one sort of discrimination that I had to put up with a lot, and that was in jobs. I wasn't allowed to take a government job. I couldn't be a nurse. There was even a law against us working for the Post Office, so it wasn't only the law in New South Wales. But oh, I could be a house cleaner all right. I could do other people's washing. I could be trusted with the keys to the house or flat when the owners were away, but actually doing what I wanted to do was out.

I was like all other Aborigines. I had black skin, and so was only good for menial kinds of jobs. The one single thing that I've always wanted to be was a nurse, so that I could help people more. I've suffered in life. I feel I have. And because of that I've been able to visit all those different kinds of people in different kinds of hospitals and, yes, gaols, and been able to understand their 'sicknesses', what they were really feeling. But no, I had the wrong colour of skin to be a nurse. So I had to teach myself whenever and however I could.

I remember, when I was about fifteen or sixteen, seeing an advertisement in a paper called *The Christian World*. It said how you could write to a publisher in London for books all about nursing and mothercraft. They were quite cheap, so I sent for them. You know, I taught myself a lot from those two books; they gave me a good enough foundation to cope with most things that came my way.

Anyway, funnily enough, I've always got on with the white people I've worked for. Many of them are still my friends. One thing I have noticed, though, is that men accepted me more than women generally. Somehow the white woman seemed to have a thing about having to *show* she was better than I was. And make it obvious, what's more. I don't know why. Could it have been jealousy? If so, jealousy of what, for heaven's sake?

I remember one white woman I worked for who asked me questions about myself. She really pried. Then she said, 'I just wanted to know, Ella, because you seem so different, so intelligent. Why don't you go away to live somewhere and marry a white man?' Well, I told her what I thought of that! I told her about some of the things I'd had to face since childhood and how I didn't want to get involved in my father-type of situation again. I wanted my family to marry their own people, too.

At least now you can talk openly about discrimination and

172

how it hurts. If we could only get our young people to make the most of their education we could show them that they have a good chance these days of getting the sorts of jobs they are capable of doing, and really want to do. I've tried to encourage them in this. I've even encouraged them to move into town, to apply for houses and learn to fit in with the town on their own terms. The old days have gone and they face a different world. They can still be proud of their Aboriginal side *and* make their way in today's world. Even at my age I've had to change my ways and not live in the past. But, you know, I don't think I'll ever stop wondering what I might have been . . .

THE END OF THE STRUGGLE

Ella Simon died on Friday, 13 February 1981; quietly and alone. Her deep concern for others and her determination to help people see 'through her eyes' continued right to the very end.

Soon after this book first appeared, she had to have another cancer operation. This was followed by more ray treatment in Sydney. She was undaunted by this and continued to think of ways she could use the time to help someone else. Her quick mind picked up some new craft ideas from other patients, and some of her Sydney friends found themselves sent off to look for the simple materials she needed. They had come to the hospital to comfort her. She was anxious to use the time between treatments to make some of these things to give them!

She was sent home. She seemed to recover and resumed her activities. She was a vital member of a nearby church; she was still deeply involved in Aboriginal affairs, even from the isolated position of the house to which she had been forced to move. Her knowledge was now much sought after, at last being accorded the respect it deserved. She was often tired, but did not ever mention how ill she really was.

Then, without telling anyone, she was admitted to

hospital for what was to be her last stay. Some of her closest relatives were, by chance, at the hospital on that Friday and found her there. She spoke to them and said goodbye as if she knew what was about to happen. They said they'd be back to see her in the morning. She just said she was very tired as she sent them away. Then she gave up the long struggle that was her life here. One result of that struggle was her very presence there in the main part of a hospital and not in the isolation ward out the back, as in her younger days. Now she was dying in the hospital proper where, as a mature woman, she'd been too afraid even to visit her dying father.

Her physician has volunteered details of the period leading up to her admission to hospital. His statement has been added in full, telling of her illness and also of her personal impact on him. (See page 187)

Ella had planned her own funeral, in detail and with much thought. It was to be both a triumphant celebration of her Christian faith and a symbolic statement of her rejection by a society which calls itself Christian. It was also finally to restate her belief in the values and ways of her Aboriginal ancestors.

Ella Simon's funeral service was an experience that the many who attended will never forget. It was more triumphant than she could possibly have envisaged. People came from great distances. It was a coming together of races and classes to honour this remarkable woman. She had chosen the hymns and instructed that she did not want a mournful service, as her life had been built on the teachings of her grandmother when Ella was only a young child. There were to be no flowers, even though she loved flowers and shared her garden with everyone. That money she wanted put to good use and the church she attended had decided on a fitting memorial to which any could contribute.

The singing would have pleased her. Singing was part of her, too. Her first hymn, 'What a friend we have in Jesus', sounded like a well-practised choral work because of the expert harmony and rhythm of the Aboriginal members

175

of the congregation and the deep feeling of everyone for this woman. A young Aboriginal group sang in appreciation of her life and her love for them.

Then the Mayor spoke of her influence in the town and his own respect for her over the thirty years he had known her. Other community leaders spoke of her helpful advice and wisdom, which they had often sought. Pastor Frank Roberts, a lifetime friend and an elected member of the National Aboriginal Conference, spoke at length of her impact on the wider Aboriginal community with her deep appreciation of what it meant to be Aboriginal. He said that though she was conservative in a lot of her views, she had the ability to get to the heart of a problem in such a way that she could stir people into really thinking. She had reminded him when he was elected to the Conference that in this high office he 'must never forget what makes our people tick'. Another statement of hers that he had never forgotten was said many years ago when he was very young. There was a very big church gathering at Lismore and in front of this crowd she'd said: 'Racial issues will always be prominent, and not only in Australia, but wouldn't it be wonderful if for just one year the church would live in the spirit of its own teaching on love in the thirteenth chapter of Corinthians'! 'We will greatly miss this dynamic and gifted lady, so full of love and social concern', he concluded.

There were statements by people who wanted to pay tribute to someone who had made such an impact on their lives. One of these was a businessman she had helped to overcome personal problems so that he could rise to his present position. Another was a young nephew with the same type of story. Part of his tribute was sung as a very moving, unaccompanied solo.

After singing the other hymn she had chosen, 'When the trumpet of the Lord shall sound', and after the Committal by the Minister, that very diverse crowd surged out to share their common grief and their experiences with Ella Simon in her lifetime. Her vision of what not only the Church but our whole society should be like came true for that brief period, when mourning made divisive issues such as skin colour, education and social position all seem as petty and trivial as they really are.

Ella had obviously thought very carefully about her burial. Not for her the pauper's burial she had so often been called upon to organise for others. Not for her the problem of where to place her grave, in which part of which cemetery; she'd had to face that one too many times, too, and the memory of her father's funeral was also deeply etched in her thinking. No, she had saved from her scarce resources and particularly from the meagre royalties from this book to pay for a cremation, which had to be at Beresfield near Maitland. Her instructions were that the cortege was to stop for a few minutes at her old home at Purfleet and then she was to continue alone to the crematorium. It was a distance of 160 kilometres and she would have been thinking of the cost for everyone; but there was also her deep feeling of not really belonging, of being alone in this world, and so she would finish her last journey alone.

So the long procession, which needed police organisation because of its size, wound its way the few kilometres to the site of her old home. The crowd stood in silence for the few minutes while prayers were said at the spot where she had known both happiness and heartache; where she had fought so many battles against the legal discrimination that had ruled her life and hurt her so deeply. Many in that funeral procession had shared that fight and that hurt; many had known very little about it until it was over. Then they all obeyed her wishes and she continued alone.

Her final instructions had been thought out over a long period and reinforced by thinking about the past for this book. In death Ella Simon was to turn away from the society that rejected her people, in spite of all she'd done, and return to her Aboriginal past. Her ashes were scattered over the old Aboriginal graves, thus bringing her life full circle and linking her beliefs and her values for the last time with those of her Aboriginal ancestors.

AFTERWORD

I had known Ella Simon most of my life. Everyone seemed
to know her in that small country town. She was that sort
of person. I did not really know her, though. I belonged to
a different world, entry to which was determined not by
personality or ability or integrity or any other accepted
virtues. It wasn't what you were that counted, but what
you looked like. A river and a few kilometres of highway
divided our worlds, but the unseen and unspoken barriers
were far greater and more impenetrable. There was neither
logic nor intelligence creating those barriers. Ella, with
bitter irony, commented while working on her book that
it was strange that our society worshipped the sun and a
suntan, often acquired at great expense, but rejected her
simply because she had one!

My early contacts with her were spasmodic. I first met
her when the local churches' youth groups were invited to
a combined gathering near her home. I later learned from
her how hard she had had to fight to get permission from
the Manager to do this. He had stood up and welcomed
everyone as if it was his own idea! There were other
meetings in the town, which probably made us feel good,
but the barriers to real friendship and fellowship were
never questioned. I cannot remember any attempt being

made to find out the true position of people like Ella. Her remarks about ignorance being the cause of prejudice apply to even the most well-meaning and sincere.

So none of us did anything to change the laws which discriminated against her and thousands like her. We didn't exactly support them, we just didn't take the trouble to find out what was happening so close to us. Most of the movement for change came from within the Aboriginal community started by people like Ella and taken up by the generations coming after her. Trade unions, some with communist members, gave financial help for legal battles; many individuals helped, but too often the Aboriginal people were left to fight their own battles against laws which should never have existed. I still have Ella's 'dog tag', the notorious Certificate of Exemption, to remind me. I did not know they existed until she showed me hers.

I lost touch after leaving the area to go to University and, like most offspring of country towns, lived and worked away in the city. When she was running the shop I often called in on my way past. She was more accessible there because it was near the highway, on the edge of what was then forbidden territory. She was a natural salesperson. She showed me how a boomerang was thrown and the different kinds, and had even mastered the art of playing the didgeridoo, which was not a local instrument. A visiting group from the Northern Territory had given her lessons. There are now several boomerangs and a didgeridoo in Scotland from that shop—with her instructions! She showed me how the local people made music with a gumleaf; they once had a gumleaf band that was quite famous.

One of these brief visits was very embarrassing. I was about to back quietly out because an officious woman was lecturing her about something. Ella was just standing there, looking very fed up but subdued. Then she spotted me and the spark returned to her eyes. With the manner of a duchess she politely interrupted the tirade and very graciously and correctly introduced her 'teacher friend

179

from Sydney' to—the Manager's wife! The tirade stopped in mid-sentence. I know now that, in those few minutes, she had won another round in the fight against the system.

Then I didn't see her for years. I was too busy building a career in the world of education. I visited my home area again before travelling a bit and then changing school systems. I was asked about some stones dug up by my brother in a newly ploughed paddock. We had heard that Ella had moved into the town, we assumed by choice, and was therefore closer and more accessible; she was the obvious one to take them to first. So we tracked her down.

She recognised the stones immediately. The yellow ones were a type of flint and she demonstrated how to make a spark and pointed out the sharp edges of the flakes. They were not local stones, but she reminded us that there had been a complex network of trade routes stretching around Australia that had existed for thousands of years before the Europeans destroyed them. She had seen the 'message sticks' carried by a member of one tribe crossing over other tribal territory. The round river stones had been flaked and she knew them to be either hand axes or reject axe-heads. 'What they made had to be perfect before they'd use them', she said, and then came one story after another to illustrate this. An innocent inquiry about whether anyone had recorded her stories brought an emphatic reply: some had started but had left the district and if anyone was going to do it 'they'd better hurry up or it will be too late'. I made a feeble offer to help.

This visit began the most extraordinary part of my education. The teacher became the student most of the time. This old lady I was supposed to be helping always seemed to be way ahead of me, even though the effort was nearly killing her. She mastered the use of a tape recorder in one lesson. The local School of Arts library lent her one to start her off. She was too impatient to wait for the Australia Council grant which eventually did come through. The idea was that she would record her story on tape. Then it would be typed and edited, following the pattern advocated by all the authorities on oral history (which is a fashionable subject at last). It is not quite as easy as it sounds!

The excellent memories of Ella's generation reproduce everyday details about which 'educated' typists and editors know nothing and, because the storyteller is old, they doubt the truth of the unusual. The 'corrections' they made wasted a lot of my time. I had set myself the task of checking for details in the State and Mitchell Libraries in Sydney because I lived there. Ella was anxious to do this, but she lived too far away. I was also constantly questioning Ella about some of her information, often to satisfy my own curiosity. Early experience had taught me to treat with respect the stories told by people like her. We spent many hours going over some details and she always had a good explanation for something unusual.

One example of the sort of detail lost in this editing had to do with the flu epidemic at the end of the First World War. She said that the young men who did recover and started to help bury the dead just dropped dead as they worked. Exaggeration? Not at all. With the current interest in epidemics, this is now well documented as the peculiar feature of that epidemic. A seemingly minor detail her acute intellect had noted and remembered was not only accurate, but also important. The editor also tried to change some of her terms. One that annoyed Ella, because of her special interest in things medical, was changing her use of the word 'antidote' to 'antivenene'. She was positive the doctor had said it was an antidote for her mother's snakebite. Another visit to the Library proved her correct; antivenenes hadn't been discovered then! Her use of the word 'law' was changed to 'lore' when she talked about Aboriginal law being the same throughout Australia despite all the different tribes and languages. She knew what she was talking about; she knew what the words meant. That one upset her because she took her role as a JP very seriously, as well as being so knowledgeable about Aboriginal law. One that took me a while to sort out was

181

when a well-meaning typist changed what was on the tape to make it sound 'correct'. She had typed that Ella's grandfather had lived 'in a monastery'. Apart from this being unlikely, there were no monasteries in those parts. She'd said, when I found it on the tape, that he'd lived 'at the Monkerai', which happens to be the name of a small district south of Gloucester in New South Wales! If the typist had kept to what the old lady had actually said, it would have taken me less time to work out than her 'correction'.

These are only a few of the examples of people 'knowing better' and these are the comparatively minor ones. Whole sections were changed, only to be changed back after more time-consuming research. It is no wonder so many misconceptions appear in books and the other media. There is obviously a great need to set the record straight, in this case about Aboriginal history and culture. If a project such as this has been subjected to so much of the 'we know better than you' attitude, we have to be very careful with what is recorded and reported—that is, if it really is truth we are seeking and not just confirmation of our own prejudices, or justification for a course of action we have already decided upon.

The legends as told by Ella had to be guarded very carefully, too. The way she told them, they made sense. They were comparable to the legends of all the other great cultures, including the various European ones. There was a purpose behind many of them and some were linked to some obvious natural feature in the local area. Others were just humorous accounts involving animals and birds whose every movement was keenly observed and cleverly wound into story and dance. She was most indignant about Aboriginal 'legends' made up by Europeans and which, to her, made the Aboriginal traditions seem inferior because they didn't make sense. She kept referring to one recorded in magnificent tiles on the wall of a bank in her own town. The first time she heard of it was when it appeared on that wall! It was supposed to tell the story of how that place got its name, but it was nothing like any local legend she'd heard. There were no serpents in any of the local stories and, besides, places were named after some important natural feature or event that had occurred there. 'Add to that a few important people's names and there's not much difference in the way places are named', she said.

The telling of her story was very costly to Ella Simon. Listening to her tell the story of her father's funeral or the death of Cecil Bungie was heartbreaking. Talking about her Certificate of Exemption, she is so angry that the words just tumble out and it is almost impossible to hear. That had to be redone several times and then left because of the traumatic effect it was having on her. In an interview with the ABC, she admitted how much it hurt her to have to remember all the things she had tried to forget, but by telling them she hoped that people would understand and the healing process would start, both with herself and with others.

Ella came to Sydney on numerous occasions. She wanted to find out a few things and see a few people. We found the records of the Aborigines Protection Board in the State Library. They are far worse than I could have believed. For me, it was like reading about another country. For her, it was seeing the official version of what had been inflicted on her for most of her life. We went to the Australia Council and then she wanted to go to the Museum. I'd kept putting off going to the Museum because it sounded crazy to ask about a bird her grandmother had talked with. In the bush this was not so strange, but this was the middle of the city! She persisted, so in we went and I heard myself making what to me was a very strange request. She then took over as we were shown into a back room where a young man didn't find her questions at all strange. He produced birds from various drawers and played tapes of birdsongs. (They were getting ready for a new display.) Those two then left me far behind in a serious discussion about bird languages. He had done post-graduate studies in the United States on the subject; her studies had been done in the Australian bush. My own post-graduate studies with Ella Simon continued.

When Ella came to stay, it was another opportunity to listen to her when she felt like talking, usually in the late afternoon. Since her move away from her old home and the death of her husband, her small television set had filled in many lonely hours so she was almost addicted to her favourite programs. There was no disturbing her while they were on. She even took a great delight in solving any crossword puzzle about television. She was a born organiser and she gradually took charge. My flat was tidier and cleaner when I got home from work; the cooking was first-class, though it meant many trips to the local shop for the exact spices or other ingredients. Even so, one of her bits of wisdom I still remember was that 'people are more important than houses'. She was apologetic about having two showers a day—as if I cared! 'It's all those years of fighting for proper bathrooms and showers', she explained. 'I still haven't got over the luxury of being able to have a good shower even after all these years.'

The hurt was still there, but it was hurt without recrimination; it wasn't directed at me, either. Her brand of practical Christianity astounded me at times. If a race of people treated me like that, could I be so completely forgiving to other members of that race?

Ella had a clear insight into the ways her Christian beliefs were built up from Aboriginal lore. This was because she had a true perspective of Aboriginal lore and found its moral and spiritual values in harmony with those of one of the world's major religions. She learned this from her grandmother early this century. It has taken longer for the students of anthropology and theology to arrive at the same conclusion after so much valuable culture has been destroyed in the name of religion or civilisation, usually by cruel force. She did criticise both systems, but it was objective criticism and she always distinguished between the organisations and the true beliefs. She had suffered under the Mission system and did not feel welcome in most of the churches; she also had valid criticisms of Aboriginal society and some tribal practices. This never altered her approach to the truth in both, and upon this she built her life.

Walking around the city with her, I was conscious of the rude stares and was upset on behalf of someone who had become a dear friend. Then I'd hear a spirited mutter from her such as, 'That lot probably think I'm a foreigner. If they look again, I might just tell them!' Then there were the quiet requests for things that for me were no real problem but which, for all her energy and drive, she would not tackle on her own. It was easier to obtain them if a white person was with her. The saddest of these requests was to go somewhere to be fitted for a prosthesis. Her cancer operation was years before that and she'd read about her needs but had never been quite game enough to ask. This was quickly solved. It only involved a visit to one of the stores in the city. Why should skin colour be so important? This human being had suffered when the answer was as simple as that. Why?

While in Sydney once, she was interviewed about bush medicines for a magazine. Her hearing was bad that day. She had bronchitis again. The journalists was talking down to her, doubting the existence of some of the plants she named and confusing her with botanical names. I realised after a while that Ella had given up and so I was left to finish the session. She was completely frustrated by this type of interview, as so many old people must be. She had so much wisdom bottled up inside her, but gave up when she was treated like this, especially if she wasn't feeling well. Other interviews were different. I remember clearly one with a linguist not long before she died. He was tapping this rich source of knowledge with the respect it deserved. She was in her element with this expert on a subject dear to her heart. He spent several days with her. I withdrew. I was out of my intellectual depth. A National Parks and Wildlife officer had a similar interview with her about place names. He had to come back when it suited her, though. He arrived in the middle of her favourite television program!

She was not easily taken in by experts. She told me

once of the anthropologists who came around and offered money to the old people to tell them stories. 'And they weren't stupid; they told them stories; they told them what they knew they wanted to hear', she said, with bitterness in her tone. She was bitter about this type of approach and because of the lost opportunities for getting at the truth for once.

Walking around the Australian bush with Ella Simon was something else. She was in control there. We heard the birds warning each other of our approach; we saw trees where possums lived; she pointed out insect life which changed with the seasons, warning the tribes that it was time to move on to ensure their food supply and build their huts before the bark was too difficult to remove in sheets; we collected specimens of the bush medicines her grandmother had used. Like most Australians, I love the bush, but I appreciated it more when I saw it through her eyes.

One of the bonuses of taking Ella around for this book was meeting people. Most of them she helped in some way; some were old people who knew the country as well as she did; there were many others as well, people from all walks of life she wanted to talk to. There were also some of her relatives that I should have been with at school. They had wanted to go on to High School. They were keen to continue their education. She had even made them the correct uniforms and bought all their gear. But the Aboriginal Welfare Board had refused them permission to go, on the grounds of the old Protection Board's law that 'if a European parent objected' they were not allowed into a school. Their education was terminated in primary school; mine continued as far as I liked. It was my choice. They had to take whatever dreary jobs they could get; I had some choice with a better education. Our abilities are the same. We share common human experiences. But there are so many lost years when they were denied the rights the rest of us take for granted. We lost all those opportunities for sharing our different cultures as well as our similarities as human beings.

When this book was first published, Ella took one of her precious four free copies all the way up to the local police station at the other end of town—quite a journey for her. She told no one of her mission. She left the copy at the front desk. Later she confided in me what she'd done. Her motive? 'If only it will help someone there to just understand; to see things through my eyes just for once.'

Seeing our world through the eyes of Ella Simon does make a difference. It can never be the same again. It is so much better; somehow bigger, deeper. Thank you, Ella.

ANNE RUPRECHT

Dr. Romney A. Newman
M.B., B.S., F.R.A.C.P. – Provider No. 103523

Dr. Louise M. Berghouse
M.B., B.S., F.R.A.C.P. – Provider No. 264551

CONSULTANT PHYSICIANS
19 YORK STREET
TAREE 2430
Telephone: 52 3162
52 3588

Dear Anne,
Re: Mrs. Ella SIMON

I was privileged to assist with the medical care of Mrs. Ella Simon during her last year. She was already aware that she had secondary breast cancer. I recall her telling me that she had asked God for two more years, during which time she wanted to see some of her family return to Him. Not long before her death, this had started to happen.

She was rather reluctant to take medications over her last few months and often attributed her symptoms to the drugs. She encouraged me to pray with her and I remember one time she stated that she preferred my prayers to my drugs. Despite these difficulties however, she was one patient who certainly encouraged me to pray with other patients and helped me understand that this was a real privilege. Praying with patients gave them an opportunity to realise they had a responsibility in the healing process, and also to realise some of the dilemmas which doctors have to face in making decisions. I saw her on her 79th birthday when she was unwell and I had actually recommended that she be admitted to hospital to see if we could improve her state. She wanted to defer this for some time but didn't tell me why. She then rang me a little over a week later to say that she was now ready to go into hospital. Within some hours of going into hospital, she died quite suddenly in the ward and obviously she had used that week to go around visiting various people as well as organising her funeral. She certainly left this world confident of where she was going.

Yours sincerely,

Romney Newman.

ROMNEY NEWMAN

INDEX